Face Recognition Technologies

Designing Systems that Protect Privacy and Prevent Bias

DOUGLAS YEUNG, REBECCA BALEBAKO,
CARLOS IGNACIO GUTIERREZ, MICHAEL CHAYKOWSKY

For more information on this publication, visit www.rand.org/t/RR4226

Library of Congress Cataloging-in-Publication Data is available for this publication.
ISBN: 978-1-9774-0455-8

Published by the RAND Corporation, Santa Monica, Calif.
© Copyright 2020 RAND Corporation
RAND® is a registered trademark.

Cover: Adobe Stock / Irina Shi.

Support RAND
Make a tax-deductible charitable contribution at
www.rand.org/giving/contribute

www.rand.org

Preface

Face recognition technologies (FRTs) offer opportunities to significantly improve identification efforts, but they also introduce concerns about privacy and bias. Understanding the trade-offs between the utility and risks of FRTs is crucial for evaluating their adoption and implementation.

This report is intended to help improve U.S. Department of Homeland Security (DHS) acquisition and oversight of FRTs by describing their opportunities and challenges. It might also be of interest to other government agencies considering how to implement FRTs and to FRT researchers and developers. Specifically, the work introduces FRT privacy and bias risks and alternatives to mitigate them.

About the Homeland Security Research Division

This research was conducted using internal funding generated from operations of the RAND Homeland Security Research Division (HSRD) and within the HSRD Acquisition and Development Program. HSRD conducts research and analysis across the U.S. homeland security enterprise and serves as the platform by which RAND communicates relevant research from across its units with the broader homeland security enterprise. For more information on the Acquisition and Development Program, see www.rand.org/hsrd or contact Emma Westerman, director of the Acquisition and Development Program, by email at emma@rand.org or phone at (703) 413-1100 ext. 5660. For more information on this publication, visit www.rand.org/t/RR4226.

Contents

Figures and Tables

Figures

Tables

Summary

Face recognition technologies (FRTs) are designed to detect and recognize people when their images are captured by a camera lens. There are many practical security-related scenarios for implementing such technology, such as for border control officers and crime scene investigators. However, these systems are not failsafe. They raise privacy and bias concerns. First, advocacy groups and the public at large have expressed concerns about privacy. Second, the systems' results can be biased in ways that harm particular ethnic and racial groups. It is important that leaders and personnel using FRTs understand the problems associated with this technology so that they can improve policies on their acquisition, oversight, and operations. Identifying privacy and bias issues inherent in an FRT system as early as possible enables the mitigation of future risks.

Homeland Security Operational Analysis Center researchers conducted an exploratory study to understand FRT-related problems with privacy and bias. Case studies and an initial literature review suggest that the U.S. Department of Homeland Security has opportunities to address these concerns in FRT design and deployments.

Understanding Two Dimensions of Face Recognition Technologies

Following an initial literature review, the researchers determined that a two-dimensional heuristic, in the form of a two-by-two matrix, is helpful in determining the accuracy of a proposed FRT (Table S.1).

Table S.1
Face Recognition Technology Use Cases, by Consent and Match Type

Consent Type	Match Type	
	Verification (One-to-One)	Identification (Some-to-Many)
Consent	• Border control passport authentication[a] • Device authentication	• Social media identity resolution • Visa screening
Nonconsent	• Law enforcement mug shots • Detainee identity verification	• Face-in-a-crowd airport surveillance[a] • Street camera surveillance • School surveillance

[a] Discussed later as a more in-depth use case.

The first dimension describes how the subject cooperates with an FRT system: with consent and without consent. In a consent scenario, the subject knows that their image is being captured and volunteers to participate. In a nonconsent scenario, the subject is not given an opportunity to reject the capture of their image. How much subjects willingly cooperate with an FRT affects its error rates. Specifically, face recognition in nonconsent scenarios is more difficult than in consent ones because of the constraints on obtaining sufficient data to extract biometric information that can identify someone.

The second dimension—match type—contrasts whether an FRT is applied for face verification or face identification. Verification is a one-to-one comparison of a reference image with another image, while identification is a search and comparison between one or many faces in a data set (which could be a database or a photo of a crowd, for example) with those in another data set. This comparison is relevant to an FRT system's bias because algorithms for one-to-one identification are currently more accurate than those for some-to-many systems.

Overall, the two-dimensional heuristic can serve as a matrix of criteria to determine whether an FRT system will be highly accurate. For example, when a consented facial image is compared with a single photo (e.g., passport), accuracy should generally be high, and the potential for privacy concerns should be low. All technological systems should be evaluated for privacy and bias, including FRT systems that might be deployed for security purposes. The heuristic illustrates the potential for privacy concerns in each of the conditions and estimated levels of accuracy, which includes the potential for bias (e.g., more false positives decreases accuracy). Yet other elements of how the FRT system is deployed and used are also important, such as the system's susceptibility to techniques intended to defeat it (hacks).

Broadly Reviewing Public Program Implementation of Face Recognition Technologies

We highlight the public programs related to the implementation of FRT or policies that discuss how biometric data are handled by entities that collect and analyze this information. Table S.2 illustrates the scope of this review.

As show in Table S.2, FRTs are being increasingly implemented in multiple sectors and across different levels of government. However, only a patchwork of laws and policies exists to govern and guide their operational use. As a result, the extent to which privacy and bias concerns can be mitigated for these implementations is limited. Addressing these gaps might require more-specific information in each of the sectors in which FRTs are deployed.

Table S.2
Selection of Policies That Govern Face
Recognition Technologies, by Sector and
Level of Government

Sector	Local	State	Federal
Schools	x	x	
Law enforcement	x	x	x
Private sector		x	x
National security			x

Examining Two Use Cases in More Detail, and Identifying Red Flags

The two use cases chosen for deeper analysis—border control passport authentication and face-in-crowd airport surveillance—involve comparable environments (airports), but they occupy opposite ends of the heuristic in Table S.1. In the first use case, feature creep beyond the one-to-one match introduces complexity to the system. This complexity introduces privacy concerns and additional issues in protecting privacy. In the second use case, additional red flags include

- Although consent and control are necessary aspects of privacy protections, the system offers no option for notice or choice.
- The base rate of potential matches is extremely low.
- Human interpretation of the results introduces additional bias and requires additional storage of full-face images or video.

We noted red flags or elements of both scenarios that can introduce privacy and bias concerns, such as **a lack of redress when errors occur** and that **the training data are a possible source of bias**. These red flags could be applied to other FRT use cases. Further analysis could extend the breadth (i.e., more use cases) and the depth (examining each use case in more detail) beyond analysis of these two use cases.

Areas for Future Research

Further research should address areas of opportunity in implementing FRTs for security purposes:

- Characterize disparate FRT privacy and bias practices at the local, state, and federal levels.
- Evaluate relevant Department of Homeland Security policies and processes.
- Identify appropriate types of and conditions for implementing privacy-enhancing technologies.

- Evaluate the privacy, bias, and hacking effects that algorithmic transparency could have on FRT implementations.
- Determine training and target data representativeness for relevant populations (e.g., travelers).
- Identify privacy and bias considerations in the government acquisition of FRTs.
- Assemble a centralized repository of FRT accuracy and implications for bias.
- Explore FRT targets' privacy expectations.

Acknowledgments

The views expressed are those of the authors. This report was written with internal funding from the Homeland Security Operational Analysis Center. We wish to thank our reviewers Don Prosnitz and Priscillia Hunt, as well as Jessie Riposo, Emma Westerman, and Isaac Porche for their feedback throughout this work. Paul S. Steinberg helped improve the clarity and coherence of this report. Kristen Hatcher, Erica Robles, and Thomas Whittaker assisted in editing and formatting this report.

Abbreviations

3-D	three-dimensional
ACLU	American Civil Liberties Union
DHS	U.S. Department of Homeland Security
DoD	U.S. Department of Defense
DOS	U.S. Department of State
FACE	Facial Analysis, Comparison, and Evaluation
FBI	Federal Bureau of Investigation
FIPP	fair information practice principle
FRT	face recognition technology
FTC	Federal Trade Commission
HIPAA	Health Insurance Portability and Accountability Act of 1996
IPS	Interstate Photo System
NGI	Next Generation Identification
NTIA	National Telecommunications and Information Administration
PET	privacy enhancing technology
PIA	privacy impact assessment

PII   personally identifiable information

CHAPTER ONE

Introduction

Humans frequently rely on the ability to recognize someone based solely on facial characteristics to determine whether they know the person, distinguish their gender or ethnicity, and decide whether to trust or interact with them. Yet those innate face recognition skills can also fail people in systematic ways. Face recognition technologies (FRTs) were designed to detect and recognize someone captured on camera. Complementing human capabilities and shortcomings, FRTs offer a digital means to assess whether a face is known and to associate it with a specific identity.

There are many practical security-related reasons for implementing such technology: Border control officers and forensic investigators (Phillips, Yates, et al., 2018), for example, have found important uses for FRT capabilities. A joint report from the Integrated Justice Information Systems Institute and the International Association of Chiefs of Police describes a wide range of law enforcement use cases for which FRTs would be beneficial, including field, investigative, and custodial and supervisory uses (Law Enforcement Imaging Technology Task Force, 2019). The report also outlines several recommendations to facilitate FRT adoption by law enforcement, including conducting public outreach and establishing best practices and principles. Other security-related scenarios include identifying a mass shooting suspect (Brandom, 2018), conducting surveillance in crowded shopping areas (Roberts, 2015) and in arenas (Draper, 2018), and identifying potential stalkers (Deb and Singer, 2018).

However, several challenges associated with FRTs can also cause concern for the public (members of which are the subjects of the technology) and users (who deploy the technology). Among the public, individuals and advocacy groups have expressed concerns related to the scope and scale of FRT data, particularly when the technology is deployed and run by a government agency. One such concern is that FRTs can increase the ease of linking biographical information to a face, thus enabling a user to link a facial image to a wide range of information, including social security number, home address, and Global Positioning System coordinates. A second public concern is that FRTs change the balance of power in human interactions; that is, they allow a user to know many individuals without a reciprocal relationship. This one-way dynamic is often referred to as *surveillance*. FRTs increase the scale of surveillance by relying not just on one person's memory but also on data sets containing information on more faces than any one human can remember. A third concern is the potential for bias. For instance, the representativeness of data used to train an FRT affects its ability to identify members of groups based on demographic characteristics. The homogeneity of these data sets has raised questions about fairness and bias in FRTs.

For users of FRTs, one of the most prominent challenges are "hacks" intended to defeat these systems. People have learned that one can defeat an FRT by donning a beard or a pair of glasses or by putting on makeup to disguise their age. Given this, in some scenarios, humans might be better suited than computers to detect certain hacks. However, as with many new technologies, problems with FRTs can arise when the technology is expected to perform better than human reasoning or assumed to fail in the same manner.

FRT adoption by government agencies can also raise societal concerns. Although government deployment of FRTs could improve public services or save lives, these benefits must be balanced with threats to privacy or civil liberties. One such risk characteristic that distinguishes government usage from, for example, private-sector usage is the perceived severity of the consequence. The government has the power to punish, jail, or limit someone's liberty; corporations lack such power. Knowledge and memory of previous government incursions on privacy and civil liberties, such as internment camps (Conrat and Conrat, 1972) and the surveillance of civil rights leaders (Garrow, 2015), might influence how members of targeted groups view the risks and benefits of FRTs.

Perceived risk of harm, which might not necessarily reflect the actual probability of harm, is an additional consideration. Multiple factors can influence a person's perception of risks, such as knowledge that an act might be risky, whether that action is undertaken voluntarily, the severity of consequences, and degree and type of personal control (whether the person can avoid harm by personal skill or diligence) (Slovic, Fischhoff, and Lichtenstein, 1980). Someone might perceive, for instance, that government implementation of FRTs encroaches on civil liberties, regardless of how it is actually deployed, and thus change their behavior accordingly.

Objectives and Approach

To help government agencies, such as the U.S. Department of Homeland Security (DHS), understand the potential problems associated with FRTs and improve policies on its acquisition, oversight, and operations of these technologies, the Homeland Security Operational Analysis Center conducted an exploratory study to understand privacy and bias concerns related to FRT implementations. Throughout this report, we discuss how to address these elements of harm—real and perceived—by increasing transparency and control over FRT use. Rather than examining what is technically feasible with FRTs, we explored actions that government agencies should consider related to their use, including how the technology can be engineered to protect privacy and reduce bias.

The research questions addressed in this report are twofold:

- How can society benefit from and use face recognition while still protecting privacy?
- What methods can be used to mitigate the disparate impact of inaccuracies in the results of using face recognition technology?

To answer the research questions, we reviewed the academic literature and current examples on privacy and bias. We conducted keyword searches of hard and social science academic databases to identify relevant studies. We then reviewed current uses of FRTs to develop two scenarios for deeper analysis.

Scope and Limitations

This report is intended as an introduction—a primer—on issues of privacy and bias in using FRT systems for government agencies that are considering how to deploy such systems. This work, therefore, aims to inform policymakers about potential broader implications of FRTs rather than provide a thorough technical review. Our literature review was not a systematic one, and we did not review government documents or interview anyone from a government agency or FRT vendor.

The two use cases focus on areas in which risk can be mitigated, but they were based largely on conjecture from open news sources about how such systems might work. Given that this effort was exploratory, we did not intend it to provide a comprehensive introduction to privacy, bias, or FRTs. As noted, we did not interview or engage anyone involved in implementing FRT systems. Such additional research would likely help to improve decisionmaking around how FRTs are implemented and deployed, but conducting it was beyond the scope of this study.

Organization of This Report

In Chapter Two, we provide a primer on FRTs, starting with two-dimensional heuristic to determine the degree to which privacy and bias issues might be present in FRT deployments. Subsequently, we provide background on how privacy and bias concerns manifest in FRTs. Chapter Three broadly discusses public policies related to the implementation of FRTs and how biometric data are handled by entities that collect and analyze this information. Chapter Four describes two use cases in which FRT systems are deployed and highlights "red flags" that suggest when FRT deployments might warrant additional consideration in terms of privacy and bias. Finally, Chapter Five provides a brief overview of the findings and some suggestions for future research.

CHAPTER TWO

Background on Face Recognition Technology: A Primer

Much like fingerprint and iris recognition, FRTs are a type of biometric identification system that relies on pattern recognition to match faces in a given data set. In other words, digitized information about a person's body (in this case, the face) is extracted from images or video and linked to other images of faces or to additional biographical information. In light of these capabilities, this chapter introduces a two-dimensional heuristic to characterize the accuracy/privacy trade-off in FRTs. It is followed by a discussion of this technology's impact on privacy (including existing methods to avoid detection or impersonate someone—usurp their identity—through hacks) and bias.

A Heuristic to Determine Trade-Offs in Accuracy and Privacy of Face Recognition Technologies

Throughout this report, we use the term accuracy to refer to an FRT's ability to compare images and correctly identify a person. This definition was selected because we wanted to follow the taxonomy used by government agencies that test (Phillips, Yates, et al., 2018) and implement (DHS, 2019) FRTs. We also recognized that FRT performance accuracy consists of multiple aspects: maximizing true positives (i.e., correctly identifying matches) and minimizing false positives (i.e., incorrectly identifying matches) and false negatives (i.e., failing to identify matches). Each of these has implications for privacy and bias.

Following a review of the literature, we identified a two-dimensional heuristic to contrast the potential privacy concerns and implications for FRT accuracy. The first dimension describes the degree to which a subject is aware of the FRT system and has agreed to cooperate with its use: with consent or without consent. In a consent scenario, a subject knows that their image is captured and cooperates by volunteering information. This leads to higher-quality images because a subject stands still, removes face coverings, and looks squarely at the camera. In contrast, in a nonconsent scenario, the subject is not given an opportunity to reject the capture of their image. In such cases, it is common to obtain obstructed views or variations in pose that reduce the FRT's accuracy (Medioni et al., 2007).

The second dimension of the heuristic contrasts face verification with identification (S. Li and Jain, 2011). Face verification is a *one-to-one* comparison of a reference image of a face with that of another face, that of someone claiming an identity. Face identification, on the other hand, involves a search of two data sets (either of which could be a database or the image of a crowd). It can search the faces in one data set for one face in the other data set (one-to-many identification, such as searching a fingerprint database for a match with fingerprints of someone just brought into custody), or it can search for any number of records from one data set in the other data set (many-to-many identification, such as surveillance cameras). In this report, we group one-to-many and many-to-many identification into a single category: *some-to-many* (although performance can differ according to use case among match types). This dimension is relevant to the FRT system's accuracy and bias because algorithms for one-to-one identification are currently more accurate than those for many-to-many identification (Liu et al., 2015).

The matrix shown in Table 2.1 can help us evaluate the potential interaction of errors with privacy and bias. For example, it suggests that use cases in the top left quadrant (one-to-one verification with consent) will likely have higher accuracy than use cases in the lower right quadrant (some-to-many identification without consent). Therefore, this two-dimensional classification can be used as a set of criteria to determine whether an FRT system will be highly accurate. In Chapter Four, we dig deeper into the opposite ends of the dimensions—border control passport authentication and face-in-a-crowd airport surveillance.

Table 2.1
Face Recognition Technology Use Cases, by Consent and Match Type

Consent Type	Match Type	
	Verification (One-to-One)	Identification (Some-to-Many)
Consent	• Border control passport authentication[a] • Device authentication	• Social media identity resolution • Visa screening
Nonconsent	• Law enforcement mug shots • Detainee identity verification	• Face-in-a-crowd airport surveillance[a] • Street camera surveillance • School surveillance

[a] See Chapter Four for a more detailed discussion.

Privacy and Privacy-Enhancing Technologies

Privacy Rights and Preferences

For this study, we define *privacy* as a person's ability to control information about themself. Its importance to individuals and countries is undeniable. According to the United Nations Declaration of Human Rights, privacy is a human right (United Nations General Assembly, 1948). Its protection can play a role in the balance of power between nations (Z. Davis and Nacht, 2018), and it is considered to be a protected civil liberty.

In practice, the concept of privacy can be difficult to implement because of context (Barth et al., 2006; Nissenbaum, 2009). DHS, for instance, has noted that it is authorized to collect biometric information from "applicants for admission into the United States claiming to be U.S. citizens and [Visa Waiver Program] travelers entering the United States" (DHS, 2016a, p. 6). However, according to a report from the Center on Privacy and Technology at Georgetown University Law Center, Congress has "never clearly authorized the border collection of biometrics from American citizens using face recognition technology" (Rudolph, Moy, and Bedoya, 2017, p. 3).

Concern about privacy—in particular, protection from surveillance—can cause people to alter their behavior. When asked,

U.S. respondents say they want and are concerned about privacy (Madden and Rainie, 2015). European Union respondents who more strongly distrust institutions (e.g., government, businesses) have a stronger preference for privacy (Patil et al., 2015). News reporting about government surveillance in the United States might have had a chilling effect (see, e.g., Schauer, 1978) on journalist speech (Bass, 2013), online behavior (Penney, 2016), and religious expression (Watanabe and Esquivel, 2009). Research on the long-term effects of surveillance find that, even though people can adapt to invasive surveillance, they find it to be a cause of "annoyance, concern, anxiety, and even rage" (Oulasvirta et al., 2012, p. 49). In one study, subjects even gave up preferred activities and hobbies to exhibit some form of control over what surveillers could see (Palen and Dourish, 2003). Moreover, surveillance is not guaranteed to result in good behavior or to deter bad behavior. For instance, the effectiveness of closed-circuit television on crime varies by context (Lim and Wilcox, 2017; Welsh and Farrington, 2009).

Consent for Data Collection and Sharing

Given the public's concerns about privacy and surveillance, obtaining consent is an important consideration in determining how FRTs are implemented. Using FRTs on people who have not consented to provide their information, either to be collected or later shared, can have negative short- and long-term effects. It can lead to less accurate or misinterpreted results, such as being included in a blacklist that denies a person's rights (e.g., air travel). Given that this collected information is generally not made publicly available (e.g., government no-fly lists, proprietary insurance risk calculations), people involved in false-positive cases might not be informed why they have been flagged, thus denying them the access to redress or grievance mechanisms (such as the legal system) to contest and resolve misunderstandings.

FRTs can also be used to provide some benefit (e.g., physical access to a facility or border entry). If someone requesting that benefit has not consented to having a photo taken, they would not have a face photo that could be used to make a successful match. For example, some travel requires a passport; if someone wanting to make such a trip never applies or provides a photo meeting the requirements to apply for a passport, they would not have consented to having a photo in the data set against which passports are checked and would therefore be denied access to that trip.

Privacy-Enhancing Technologies

In deploying new technologies, particularly in security contexts, government agencies might need to consider the inherent trade-off between protecting privacy and providing security. The field of privacy engineering, which has grown in recent years, addresses opportunities to build privacy protection into software and hardware (Dennedy, Fox, and Finneran, 2014). We explored privacy engineering to identify ways to reap the security benefits of FRT while still building privacy into security-focused systems. Although privacy engineering encompasses a variety of tools and techniques, we focused on three opportunities for its implementation on FRT systems:

- **Data protection** focuses on protecting existing data by using encryption or by separating system roles or tasks. This ensures the integrity of the data and that only intended and authorized viewers can read the information. It is specifically useful in preventing malicious attempts to gather information.
- **Data minimization, reduction, and anonymization** focus on reducing the amount of information available, even to authorized users. Examples of relevant methods include differential privacy and k-anonymization (J. Davis and Osoba, 2016).[1]
- **Data transparency and correctability** are access and control techniques that emphasize that subjects (e.g., travelers) have a role in determining and understanding how their data are handled. Sophisticated user access and control options for privacy include providing the public with notice (helping potential subjects understand what information about them is used and how it is

---

[1] Each of these techniques aims to obfuscate identifying information about individuals in a database while ensuring that the database is still useful for analysis. Differential privacy accomplishes this by adding statistical "noise" to the data, while k-anonymization clusters data into groups in which group members cannot be distinguished from each other.

used) and choice (granting control over the flow of information) (Cranor, 2012). Furthermore, opportunities should be available to correct information if needed. Despite the availability of notice and choice, individuals' control over their data might ultimately depend on how a government agency chooses to balance privacy and security.

The first two opportunities—data protection and data minimization, reduction, or anonymization—lie only within the control of the system implementer and developers. Those whose faces are being matched will have little to no opportunity to affect privacy in those cases. Data transparency and correctability must also be built by system developers and implementers, but these techniques provide more opportunity for the subject (e.g., traveler) to understand and correct data held and used about themself.

Face Recognition Hacks

One way people try to preserve their privacy is by "hacking" FRTs. FRTs are not immune to efforts to undermine their effectiveness through a variety of attack vectors. Depending on the intention of whoever performs these acts, they can be viewed as a means to either protect privacy by making it difficult for cameras to scan one's face (detection avoidance) or facilitate illegal acts by falsifying one's facial characteristics (impersonation). This section describes techniques to hack FRTs with the intention of either detection avoidance or impersonation.

Detection Avoidance

Also known as dodging or biometric obfuscation, detection avoidance can increase the variation between subjects' physical appearance and the collection of images used to identify them (Dhamecha et al., 2014; Sharif et al., 2016). Currently, almost all variations of detection avoidance techniques rely on the temporary or permanent physical modification or concealment of facial features.

Temporary techniques, such as the placement of socially acceptable barriers (e.g., scarves) or false facial hair (e.g., mustaches and beards), can degrade an FRT system's ability to detect a matching identity (Min, Hadid, and Dugelay, 2014; Zhuang et al., 2013). Several studies have highlighted the role of glasses in detection avoidance. Subjects whose identification pictures include glasses are more likely to evade FRTs once they take them off (the "Clark Kent effect") (Moniz et al., 2010). Glasses can also be designed to mislead FRTs by using specific color patterns, by being built with materials that absorb and reflect natural light in novel ways, or by emitting infrared light that blinds camera systems (Jozuka, 2015; Sharif et al., 2016). A drawback of the light-emitting method is that it might attract the attention of authorities because it would immediately raise awareness that someone is attempting to avoid identification.

Applying temporary or permanent makeup can also decrease the effectiveness of FRTs (Guo, Wen, and Yan, 2014; Moeini, Faez, and Moeini, 2015). Guodong Guo and his colleagues created a taxonomy that describes how applying makeup creates contrast in a person's facial characteristics (Guo, Wen, and Yan, 2014). The taxonomy includes skin color tone, alteration of which can be used to modify a person's apparent race; skin smoothness and texture, modification of which can alter the appearance of scars, pimples, and wrinkles; and skin highlights, which can accentuate different elements of a face.

Cosmetic surgery is a technique that permanently alters someone's features and challenges the accuracy of FRTs (Moeini, Faez, and Moeini, 2015; Nappi, Ricciardi, and Tistarelli, 2016). It can be performed locally (on a single facial feature) or globally (complete facial reengineering) (Ali et al., 2016). The ability to correctly identify someone who has undergone plastic surgery can vary significantly based on the FRT methodology and the type of surgery (Nappi, Ricciardi, and Tistarelli, 2016). For instance, identification rates after an otoplasty (ear surgery) range from approximately 56 percent to 90 percent, while identification rates after a skin peeling can go from approximately 5 percent to 95 percent (Nappi, Ricciardi, and Tistarelli, 2016).

Impersonation

Impersonation or spoofing is the act of reducing the facial differences between an impostor and a target (Akhtar and Foresti, 2016; Dhamecha et al., 2014; Köse and Dugelay, 2014). Its intent could be to access a system or to mislead authorities into believing that a target is present at several locations at once. Although techniques can be similar to those used for detection avoidance, impersonation appears to be the more challenging to accomplish (Sharif et al., 2016). Research on this topic describes four techniques to spoof an identity: photograph, video, masks, and morphing (Lai and Tai, 2016; Määttä, Hadid, and Pietikäinen, 2012; Zhang et al., 2018).

Photograph

Photograph spoofing is the most prevalent technique because of how easy and inexpensive it is (Cho and Jeong, 2017; Kose and Dugelay, 2014). It requires merely that a user obtain the target's photograph and present it to an FRT system (Cho and Jeong, 2017). Drawbacks to this approach include the absence of three-dimensional (3-D) information and the presence of vibrations caused by the hand holding the picture (Kose and Dugelay, 2014; Parveen et al., 2015). In addition, a photograph is unlikely to emulate certain characteristics of a living person, such as eye and mouth movement, known in the literature as "liveness." One method of countering this drawback is to cut eye and mouth holes, which enables an impersonator to endow the picture with "natural" movements (Kollreider, Fronthaler, and Bigun, 2008).

Video

High-quality video of a target shown on a high-resolution screen is an alternative to photos in an impersonation hack. Unlike those in photographs, facial features in a video are unlikely to be static. If an FRT system incorporates liveness in its verification of identity, a video of a person blinking, performing facial expressions, and breathing is useful for validation (Määttä, Hadid, and Pietikäinen, 2012). However, these benefits rely on obtaining video footage in which facial characteristics are clearly visible (Edmunds and Caplier, 2018).

Masks

The most challenging spoofing technique is constructing and presenting a 3-D mask. The evolution of 3-D scanning and printing techniques has supplied the tools necessary to facilitate the production of this type of impersonation hack. The main issue that impersonators face is that gaining access to the information needed to build an accurate representation is virtually impossible without the target's cooperation (Edmunds and Caplier, 2018). Some FRT systems interact with subjects by requesting a series of movements or a motion password, which the mask technique can defeat (Cho and Jeong, 2017). Adding other biometric identification (such as gait or speech verification) to the FRT can likely counter this hack.

Morphing

The last type of attack is known as morphing, in which a picture of an individual is combined with that of similar-looking person (L. Li, Correia, and Hadid, 2018). In their study, Robertson, Kramer, and Burton posited a scenario in which someone updates their government identification with a morphed picture of two people so that both of those subjects can use the new document. In their preliminary tests, humans accept a morphed identification 68 percent of the time, while a commercially available FRT (from a mobile phone) accepted it 27 percent of the time (Robertson, Kramer, and Burton, 2017).

Bias in Face Recognition

Bias is a growing concern in machine learning in general and for face recognition in particular (Barocas and Selbst, 2016; Lerman, 2013; Osoba and Welser, 2017). Bias consists of unjustified trends that favor or disfavor one group over another. Of particular concern is illegal, unethical, and undesirable bias against certain groups of people. Minorities and groups who believe they might be out of step with the majority or other scrutinized communities might avoid openly engaging in speech or other behaviors (Electronic Frontier Foundation, undated). In FRTs, bias can be perpetuated by physical facial characteristics, such as eye shape or skin color. Well-known examples of algorithmic bias exist across diverse policy areas, such as criminal justice (e.g., Angwin et al., 2016) and disease surveillance (e.g., Google, undated; Lazer et al., 2014). Biased FRT results can lead to a variety of potential harms—lack of consent, targeting of population groups, measurement error, and deliberate targeting—which we discuss in the next section.

Targeting of Population Groups (Training and Target Data)

Given that FRTs typically rely on algorithms that are "trained" with data to focus on specific characteristics, different configurations and operational approaches can disproportionately affect population groups when performing FRT "targeting" actions. In this section, we discuss these two intersecting processes.

Training Data

Commonly used to program FRTs, *supervised learning* techniques rely on manually prelabeled data to "teach" algorithms the characteristics on which they should focus their attention. Thus, bias in the training data (the inputs) can result in biased outputs. For example, if a set of facial photos contains disproportionately few people of a given race or with a specific facial characteristic, the FRT algorithm will never "learn" to recognize them.

Research suggests that demographic skew in training data can affect FRTs' performance in identifying people. One such analysis explored the role of demographic information in a set of commercially available FRT tools (Klare et al., 2012). The results indicated that female, black, and younger faces were consistently misidentified. In particular, racial bias in FRT is known as "the other-race effect," after similar findings that humans are better able to recognize faces of their own race (Phillips, Jiang, et al., 2011). Comparing algorithms developed with training data that centered on either Western or East Asian countries, Phillips and colleagues found that the algorithms matched more white or East Asian faces, respectively. Indeed, multiple reports have found that many FRTs have poor recognition of black faces (Rudolph, Moy, and Bedoya, 2017; Lynch, 2018). In another study, researchers found that three commercial FRTs that focus on gender classification—Microsoft Cognitive Services, IBM Watson, and Face++—performed best on men and lighter-skinned people (Buolamwini and Gebru, 2018). These FRTs performed worst on darker-skinned women. The study authors also concluded that several public facial image data sets disproportionately contained many light-skinned and fewer dark-skinned faces and, in particular, fewer dark-skinned female faces.

Targeting Data

After an FRT is trained, it is applied to target data—a data set of labeled or identified face images, which, given a subject image or set of images, the FRT searches for potential matches. An important consideration is the origin and thus composition of this data set. For instance, a face data set might be intended either to represent a targeted population of interest (e.g., suspected criminals or terrorists) or to consist of faces drawn from the general public (e.g., closed-circuit television stills, driver's license photos). Paradoxically, the risk of biased results might be greater when more-limited reference data sets are used. If, for example, the face data set contains mug shots, racial bias in arrest rates could result in skewed demographics in mug shots. This would increase the likelihood that facial match rates would be disproportionately high among racial and ethnic groups that were disproportionately represented in the reference data set. As a result, this would harm people in the overrepresented group by subjecting them to unwarranted scrutiny, and it would harm the broader public for whom an implementation (e.g., security-related) was intended to protect. Indeed, targeting data can overrepresent certain groups. For example, mug shot databases might contain disproportionately more black faces because of disproportionate arrest rates (Garvie, Bedoya, and Frankle, 2016).

The demographic composition of nonmatched facial images in the target data set—in other words, the "background" against which matched images exist—can also influence algorithm performance (O'Toole et al., 2012). Finally, although FRT accuracy improves with larger amounts of training data, it declines as the size of the target data set increases (Kemelmacher-Shlizerman et al., 2016).

Measurement Error

FRTs are built on algorithms that compare facial images and estimate the likelihood of matches. Although such computer-based techniques might be assumed to be infallible—or at least less susceptible to bias than humans are—in fact, algorithms can harbor hidden biases that reflect the experiences, characteristics, and even preferences of their human creators (Osoba and Welser, 2017). For instance, an algorithm might be written to assign undue weight to, omit, or misinterpret certain data features in its model. Moreover, these choices can be completely unknown. Inadvertent or intentional harm can result because the algorithms are opaque or lack transparency about which features are used to identify and match faces.

Deliberate Targeting

Much of the debate about ensuring fairness in FRT revolves around removing unintended bias. But algorithms or data sets could deliberately introduce bias into FRTs by being developed such that the results correlate on race. In a non-FRT example, Tufekci raised the possibility that algorithm-based hiring could be based on commuting distance; although commuting distance might be a seemingly innocuous measure, it could exploit extreme residential segregation that exists in the United States (Tufekci, 2015). Similar algorithms used for FRTs could skew the results toward disproportionately including or excluding certain groups, such as to advance ideological agendas or exploit political polarization to destabilize societies.

Summary

All technological systems should be evaluated for privacy and bias, including FRT systems that might be deployed for security purposes. The heuristic proposed in this chapter offers a means of identifying privacy and bias concerns. Summarizing the information presented in this chapter, Figure 2.1 illustrates the potential for privacy concerns in each of the conditions and estimated levels of accuracy, which includes the potential for bias (e.g., more false positives decreases accuracy).[2] For example, when a consented facial image is compared with a single

---

[2]   In other words, low accuracy is necessary but not sufficient to suggest the presence of bias. However, the potential for bias suggests decreased accuracy.

Figure 2.1
Accuracy and Privacy Trade-Offs in Face Recognition Technology

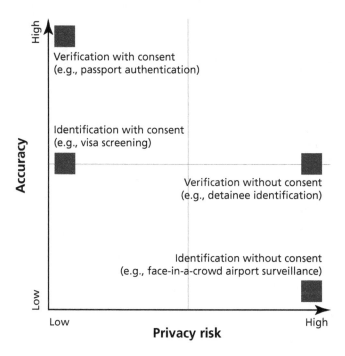

photo (e.g., passport), accuracy should generally be high, and the potential for privacy concerns should be low.

Yet other elements of how the FRT system is deployed and used are also important, such as the system's susceptibility to techniques intended to defeat it ("hacks"). Chapter Four presents greater detail on these elements in two use cases. Through these use-case "deep dives," we identify red flags that could signal the need for privacy-enhancing technologies (PETs) or bias-reduction strategies.

CHAPTER THREE

Selected Face Recognition Technology Policies in the United States

In this chapter, we highlight selected public policies and laws that constrain or guide the use of FRTs. In doing so, we also briefly describe some FRT programs and applications that might be affected or governed by these policies. This is intended to show some of the considerations that shape how FRTs are used, particularly at different levels or in different sectors of government. The information herein is not meant as an exhaustive account of every FRT-related public program or policy. Rather, it is a compilation of sectors in which this technology is applied to identify or surveil people. Table 3.1 presents the jurisdiction that different levels of government have over the sectors considered in this section: schools, law enforcement, the private sector, and national security.

Table 3.1
Selected Policies That Currently Govern Face Recognition Technology Programs, by Sector and Level of Government

Sector	Level of Government		
	Local	State	Federal
Schools	x	x	
Law enforcement	x	x	x
Private sector		x	x
National security			x

Schools

In the wake of violent incidents in schools throughout the United States, local districts have considered installing FRT systems to improve the security of staff and students. The objectives for such systems vary from managing the entry of adults into buildings (one-to-many matching) to warning administrators of the presence of people who could represent a risk (some-to-many matching). Specifically, the latter type of systems is designed to identify people in data sets of sex offenders, expelled students, and former employees. As an added benefit—one not related to face recognition per se—some systems are also capable of detecting the presence of guns.

An example of a one-to-many system being tested is called SAFR ("secure, accurate facial recognition") by RealNetworks. It is a software-based solution currently implemented in a Seattle school that works with existing hardware and verifies the identities of teachers and parents who have opted into the program (Lapowsky, 2018). The developer provides no information about the accuracy of its software, and all considerations about the security, privacy, and consent of the data gathered from participants are left up to each school (RealNetworks, 2018).

Other approaches do not contemplate a consent mechanism through which users can opt in. Several school districts either are planning or have already invested resources to install many-to-many FRT systems. For instance, in its latest "Safety and Security Master Plan," the Fort Bend Independent School District in Texas proposes a system that would identify unauthorized individuals on campus and use a mobile phone application to alert students and staff (Fort Bend Independent School District, 2019; McClellan, 2018). A district in New York, Lockport City, used a state grant of $4 million to purchase 300 FRT-capable cameras and equipment for eight schools that would alert district officials when someone found in any of a variety of data sets or someone with an open-carry permit for a weapon was detected (Fenster, 2018; Schanz, 2018). Authorities in Lockport City argued that such a system would enhance security and the utility of its existing camera infrastructure because the system was, at that time, used only to review events after they happened (Schanz, 2018). Similarly, the

Magnolia School Board in Arkansas purchased more than 200 cameras at a cost of $300,000 for a system with capabilities comparable to those of the system in Lockport City ("Magnolia School District Buying Advanced Camera Surveillance Technology for MHS," 2018).

As to privacy and data security, each school district is charged with determining how its FRT system will be used. In the case of Lockport City, authorities in the New York State Education Department approved the use of the FRT system and assured the public that data would not be shared with third parties and that all the video collected would be subject to the school district's "data use and storage policies" (Schanz, 2018). Groups that monitor civil liberties and rights, such as the American Civil Liberties Union (ACLU), have requested further information in several of these districts. Such groups are interested in detailed information about who has access to the logs of the FRT system (private parties; local, state, or federal government officials) and whether images will be used for other activities (such as immigration enforcement) (ACLU of Arkansas, 2018; ACLU of New York, 2018).

Scarce evidence exists about how effective FRT systems are in a school setting. Administrators value the advantage provided by active video surveillance that is capable of automating a process that would otherwise require substantial resources to complete. Nevertheless, some have observed that violent incidents in schools tend to be carried out by students with the right to be on campus (Juvonen, 2001). Thus, an FRT system aimed at identifying people who lack permission to be on school property might have limited value in protecting these communities (Strauss, 2018).

Law Enforcement

Law enforcement agencies at all levels of government have adopted FRTs for two purposes: to verify (confirm) an identity or identify (recognize) an unknown person (Garvie, Bedoya, and Frankle, 2016). At the local and state levels, these institutions have a degree of autonomy in determining their data privacy policies (Global Justice Information Sharing Initiative, 2017).

One effort to examine this variation is Georgetown University Law Center's Center on Privacy and Technology study, "The Perpetual Line-Up," on the use of FRTs by the 50 largest law enforcement agencies in the country (Garvie, Bedoya, and Frankle, 2016). Figure 3.1 presents a sample of its results, which reflect multiple aspects evaluated from a department's FRT policy. High marks in *accuracy* indicate agencies that have done most of the following: tested their algorithms with the National Institute of Standards and Technology, have contracts with vendors that stipulate that tests for accuracy will be performed in the future, have humans involved in validating the results of queries, and use FRT results "as investigative leads only." Agencies that had performed slightly fewer of these activities were described as "medium accuracy," while those that performed the fewest were described as "low accuracy." In terms of *consent to appear* in these data sets, entities with high marks include only mug shots of arrested individuals and exclude images from cases in which there was a not-guilty verdict or in which no charges were filed. Medium-ranking departments included mug shots of arrested individuals but removed a mug shot only when the person had applied for and been granted expungement. Low-ranking departments include in their databases all mug shots and photos from driver's license records. High-ranking departments in the field of *public transparency* have FRT policies reviewed by legislative agencies or civil liberty groups. Medium-ranking departments in public transparency also had FRT policies but those policies had not been reviewed or approved. Low-ranking departments had no such policy that was publicly available.

At the federal level, two laws govern the collection of personal information: the Privacy Act of 1974 (Pub. L. 93-579; U.S. Department of Justice, 2015) and the E-Government Act of 2002 (Pub. L. 107-347; U.S. Department of Justice, 2014). They mandate that government programs notify the public about the collection, disclosure, and use of personal information through a system-of-records notice and privacy impact assessments (PIAs). The Federal Bureau of Investigation (FBI) maintains two databases that apply FRTs. The first is a database of more than 30 million images of faces, representing about 16.9 million people (U.S. Government Accountability Office, 2016). Called the

Figure 3.1
Selected Results from "The Perpetual Line-Up"

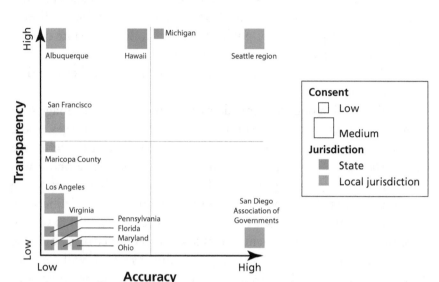

SOURCE: Garvie, Bedoya, and Frankle, 2016.
NOTE: Consent: high = The database contains "[m]ug shots of individuals arrested, with enrollment limited based on the underlying offense, and/or with mug shots affirmatively 'scrubbed' by police to eliminate no-charge arrests or not-guilty verdicts." Medium = The database contains "[m]ug shots of individuals arrested, with no limits or rules to limit which mug shots are enrolled, or where mug shots are removed only after the individual applies for, and is granted, expungement." Low = The database contains "[d]river's license photos in addition to mug shots of individuals arrested."
Transparency: high = "Agency has a public face recognition use policy that has been reviewed or approved by a legislature and/or privacy and civil liberties groups." Medium = "Agency has a public use policy, but there is no evidence the policy received external review or approval." Low = "Agency has not made its use policy public, or has no use policy."
Accuracy: high = "Agency demonstrates four or five criteria." Medium = "Agency demonstrates three of the criteria." Low = "Agency demonstrates two or fewer of the criteria." The criteria are as follows: "Algorithms have been tested by the National Institute of Standards and Technology; [c]ontract with vendor company contains provisions that require face recognition algorithms to have been tested for accuracy and will be tested at all future opportunities; [m]ost or all face recognition queries are validated by trained human examiners or agencies have a unit or designated personnel that perform a review and screening function of the candidate lists (weighted as two criteria); [and] [f]ace recognition results or candidate lists are treated as investigative leads only."

Next Generation Identification (NGI) Interstate Photo System (IPS), this database consists of both criminal mug shots and civilian pictures from varied sources, such as forms from "applicants, employees, licensees, and those in positions of public trust" (FBI, 2015). A state or government agency can submit a face image to the FBI, which will then return the top 50 matches, along with fingerprint and other identifying information.

This FRT is a one-to-many identification system: One image submitted by the state agency is compared with 30 million images, and a set of best matches is returned. The images in the database might have been gathered cooperatively; for example, a driver's license photo will consist of someone sitting in front of a camera and (likely) respecting the requirements of the photo (as opposed to walking by or deliberately trying to obscure the image). However, in this case, the FBI is storing these images and making them available for a secondary use. Someone cooperating with capturing the image for a driver's license will consider the primary use to be that of state identification and might expect it to be used to identify themself to law enforcement (e.g., at a traffic stop). However, they might be unaware that their images can be added to a collection of mug shots to be probed in law enforcement investigations as stipulated by a system-of-records notice or PIA published by the relevant government agency.

The PIA for the NGI IPS details key pieces of information about the privacy, accuracy, and consent of subjects whose pictures are included in the database (FBI, 2015). One of them is that access to pictures is limited to authorized law enforcement users whose identity and search results are preserved. Results may be used only to aid an investigation, not for positive identification. In keeping with standards by the National Archives and Records Administration, a picture can be destroyed either when the subject reaches 110 years of age or seven years after the administration receives notification of the subject's death. In terms of consent, anyone whose civilian photo is requested because of licensing or employment may refuse to submit their picture, but this might affect their ability to comply with the regulations of agencies managing these processes. Conversely, someone whose picture is obtained through arrest is unable to decline to participate in this database. Finally, in terms of accuracy, the FBI has determined that, in 85 percent of cases in which at least 50 results are found, at least one picture of the subject will be included (U.S. Government Accountability Office, 2016).

The second database maintained by the FBI is the Facial Analysis, Comparison, and Evaluation (FACE) service; its use is limited to the bureau's own investigations. The main difference between the two databases is that FACE has access to criminal photos from law enforcement and images from external partners, such as the U.S. Department of Defense (DoD), the consular database for the U.S. Department of State (DOS), and photos of criminal and noncriminal subjects from 16 states, totaling more than 411 million pictures (U.S. Government Accountability Office, 2016). Privacy standards similar to those mentioned for the NGI IPS database apply to FACE.

Throughout government, the procurement of FRT depends on software and hardware provided by the private sector. Recently, several companies have publicly acknowledged concerns about this technology's effects on civil liberties. Some have chosen to advocate for stronger privacy protections at the national level, while others have decided not to offer their solutions to law enforcement agencies (Amazon Web Services, undated; Smith, 2018; Walker, 2018). Then again, the threat to civil rights has motivated policymakers in San Francisco and Massachusetts to pursue a moratorium on FRTs in all government agencies under their control (City and County of San Francisco, 2019; Commonwealth of Massachusetts Senate, 2019b).

Private Sector

Firms in many sectors of the economy are taking advantage of FRTs to provide innovative services to consumers and organizations. Technology companies have released devices, such as the Apple iPhone X, that use face recognition for authentication processes (one-to-one). Google and Facebook analyze uploaded images in an attempt to match subjects to their databases of images from more than 2 billion active users (one-to-many). Other commercial FRT products have been marketed and sold as surveillance tools for government agencies, such as Amazon's Rekognition and Panasonic's FacePRO. Rekognition, in particular, has attracted criticism from civil rights groups for its use by law enforcement (Dwoskin, 2018). Yet FRT use by the private sector in the United States is not governed under a homogeneous set of rules. Instead, different levels of government have established guidelines for how facial images are procured, analyzed, and commercialized.

At the federal level, biometric information is protected under the jurisdiction of legislation distributed in selected sectors and demographics (Table 3.2). For example, an image of a child's face under the Children's Online Privacy Protection Act of 1998 (Pub. L. 105-277, Title XIII) or an identifiable picture in an electronic medical record under the Health Insurance Portability and Accountability Act of 1996 (HIPAA) is considered protected personal information (Federal Trade Commission [FTC], 2015; Means et al., 2015). Applications of FRT that fall outside the scope of laws in Table 3.2 are not federally protected.

At the state level, Illinois, Washington, and Texas have enacted legislation that specifically targets private-sector use of biometric information, such as facial images. California has also passed similar legislation that goes into effect in 2020 (State of California, 2018). A common thread of this legislation is defining biometric identifiers that encompass facial images by describing them as "face geometry" or unique biological patterns that identify a person (Illinois Compiled Statutes, 2008; 11 Tex. Bus. & Com. Code § 503.001; Washington State Legislature, 2017). Another point of emphasis is the onus on a firm to provide notice and procure consent for any commercial use of an identifying image. Finally, firms must take reasonable care against third-party access of these data and establish finite retention periods.

One of the main differences between these states' laws is the entity empowered to enforce them. In Texas and Washington, only the state attorney general is charged with this role. In California, the state attorney general and the consumer share responsibility for taking action against entities that violate privacy protections. However, in Illinois, any person has the right to pursue action against firms and obtain damages between $1,000 and $5,000 per violation. As a result, such

Table 3.2
Examples of Federal Laws Regulating Collection, Use, and Storage of Personal Information

Area	Authority
Health	**HIPAA** governs the disclosure of individually identifiable health information collected by covered health care entities and sets standards for data security.
Children	The **Children's Online Privacy Protection Act** of 1998 (Pub. L. 105-277, Title XIII) generally prohibits the online collection of personal information from children under 13 without verifiable parental consent.
	The **Family Educational Rights and Privacy Act** (created by Pub. L. 93-380, 1974, § 513, as amendments to the General Education Provisions Act) governs the disclosure of PII from education records.
Trade	The **FTC** is charged with setting regulations and prosecuting unfair and deceptive trade practices. Most enforcement related to the protection of private information is relegated to the enforcement of voluntary privacy policies enacted by firms.
Credit	The **Fair Credit Reporting Act** (created by Pub. L. 91-508, 1970, Title VI, as amendments to the Consumer Credit Protection Act) governs the disclosure of personal information collected or used for eligibility determinations for such things as credit, insurance, or employment.
Electronic communications	The **Electronic Communications Privacy Act** (Pub. L. 99-508, 1986) prohibits the interception and disclosure of electronic communications by third parties unless a specified exception applies.
	The **Computer Fraud and Abuse Act** (Pub. L. 99-474, 1986) prohibits obtaining information from a protected computer through the intentional access of a computer without authorization or exceeding authorized access.
Financial institutions	The **Gramm–Leach–Bliley Act** (Pub. L. 106-102, 1999) governs the disclosure of nonpublic information collected by financial institutions and sets standards for data security.

SOURCE: U.S. Government Accountability Office, 2015.
NOTE: PII = personally identifiable information.

companies as Google, Facebook, and Shutterfly have been sued for collecting and tagging consumers' facial information (Neuburger, 2016; Neuburger, 2017a; Neuburger, 2017b; Neuburger, 2018). The court cases in Illinois have resulted in contentious rulings. Some cases were dismissed because firms asserted that, although they had collected biometric information, plaintiffs could not prove "concrete injuries" because of the defendants' actions (Liao, 2018; *Rivera v. Google*, 2018). However, the Illinois supreme court recently ruled that the violation of the law was a "real and significant" injury, which could open the door for further legal action (*Rosenbach v. Six Flags Entertainment Corp.*, 2019; Gold and Braun, 2019).

As of early 2019, momentum for protecting biometric information among state legislatures was increasing, with at least eight additional states introducing bills to protect biometric information: Alaska, Connecticut, Delaware, Massachusetts, Michigan, Montana, New Hampshire, and New York (Illman, 2018; see also, e.g., Alaska State Legislature, 2017; Delaware House of Representatives, 2018; Commonwealth of Massachusetts Senate, 2019a; Michigan Legislature, 2017; and New York State Assembly, 2019).

Outside of government, the nonprofit sector has also been galvanized by the discussion of protecting biometric information and its repercussions on private firms. One of the most important forums for this debate was hosted by the National Telecommunications and Information Administration (NTIA), part of the U.S. Department of Commerce. NTIA convened a forum for nonprofit organizations to reach a consensus on best practices for commercial face recognition (NTIA, 2016). Two groups of nongovernmental organizations participated in the forum (see Table 3.3 for a full list of these organizations). The first group consisted of associations of private-sector firms that represent the views and interests of those firms' shareholders to government bodies and the public. The second group consisted of organizations characterized by their advocacy for consumer rights and the public interest.

Both groups agreed on the importance of advocating for consumer protection based on fair information practice principles (FIPPs), which reflect international standards for protecting individual information and were enshrined into federal government practice through the Privacy Act of 1974 (Pub. L. 93-579; Gellman, 2019). They encompass specific practices about consent, retention of information, and access to data, among other issues relevant to PII. However, the main point of contention in debating FIPPs was whether they should be manda-

Table 3.3
Nongovernmental Groups Interested in Face Recognition Technology Policies

Entity	Remit
Private-sector associations	
International Biometrics and Identity Association	"[I]nternational trade group representing the identification technology industry"
Digital Signage Federation	"[T]he only not-for-profit independent voice of the digital signage industry"
Interactive Advertising Bureau	"[E]mpowers the media and marketing industries to thrive in the digital economy"
Consumer Technology Association	"[A]dvocates for the entrepreneurs, technologists, and innovators who mold the future of the consumer technology industry"
NetChoice	"[A] trade association of businesses who [sic] share the goal of promoting free speech and free enterprise on the net"
Consumer and public advocates	
ACLU	Works "to defend and preserve the individual rights and liberties that the Constitution and the laws of the United States guarantee everyone in this country"
Center for Democracy and Technology	"[W]ork to preserve the user-controlled nature of the internet and champion freedom of expression"
Consumer Federation of America	"[A]dvance the consumer interest through research, advocacy, and education"
Electronic Frontier Foundation	"[D]efending civil liberties in the digital world"

SOURCES: International Biometrics and Identity Association, undated; Digital Signage Federation, undated; Interactive Advertising Bureau, undated; American National Standards Institute, undated; NetChoice, undated; ACLU, undated; Center for Democracy and Technology, undated; Consumer Federation of America, undated; Electronic Frontier Foundation, undated.

tory or voluntary. The industry groups advocated for voluntary standards, by which each firm would decide how to safeguard its FRT data, while consumer groups supported mandatory best practices, potentially implemented through legislation, to protect consumers. This disagreement led several consumer rights advocacy groups to abandon the NTIA forum (NTIA, 2016).

National Security

As mentioned in the law enforcement section, national security–focused federal efforts that compile PII, including those that use FRTs, are governed by laws that require the disclosure of how their efforts affect individuals' privacy. This section highlights a variety of programs that feature this technology.

DoD and DHS have developed automated biometric identification systems to document the identities of non-U.S. individuals suspected of terrorism or considered to be a security threat to troops (DHS, 2012; U.S. Army Test and Evaluation Command, 2015; U.S. Government Accountability Office, 2017). Once information (such as a photo) is taken for a suspect, these agencies feed it into the identification system, where other federal departments can reference the information in their one-to-many searches. Because of their status, these individuals are unable to refuse consent to having their biometric information included in the system, but they are given the opportunity to redress how they are classified (DHS, 2012; DHS, 2012, appendixes).

In the United States, the implementation of FRT has centered on the immigration process. DOS has a one-to-many system capable of identifying someone in the visa application process who might pose a security concern (McKamey, 2017; Chappellet-Lanier, 2018). The system compares pictures of applicants with photos in databases that include people who were refused visas and are watch-listed by the National Counterterrorism Center (DOS, 2013; DOS, 2015). For this program, applicants submit their data voluntarily because they are attempting to obtain permission to enter the country, and the United States notifies them that their information can be stored for cross-validation of identity purposes.

DHS has increasingly adopted FRTs in its airport operations. The DHS Facial Comparison Project is a one-to-one system that validates traveler identity by comparing a traveler's face with that in a single photo (DHS, 2016b). For these FRTs, the traveler scans their microchipped e-passport in a machine for verification and has a headshot taken, for which they might be asked to remove head covers or glasses.[1] The system then uses FRT to compare the headshot with the traveler's e-passport information. This system has a few characteristics worth highlighting. First, the FRT is used to determine whether there is a match between the vetted passport photo and the picture taken at the airport. Second, it is assumed that, for both pictures (the one taken for the passport and the one taken at the airport), the person knew that their image was being taken and complied with any request to improve photo quality. Although travelers are not allowed to opt in or out, they have the ability for redress through DHS's Traveler Redress Inquiry Program, and images are retained only for those individuals who are subject to secondary inspection (DHS, 2016b). Other DHS efforts include a 2017 solicitation to create technology to identify people entering the country through land borders without subjects leaving their cars (one-to-many) (GovTribe, 2018).

Outside the realm of border control, DHS is studying vetting immigrants using social media, but there are many considerations—technical, organizational, measurement, and legal—to be resolved before such a system could be implemented. Accordingly, DHS headquarters and operational (e.g., U.S. Customs and Border Protection) components have begun efforts to expand DHS's ongoing use of social media to accomplish a key mission: screening and vetting people seeking entry into the United States (DHS, 2017). Part of the desired analytic capabilities include face recognition, which is important for identity resolution—that is, determining that someone is who they say they are. DHS considered this question a crucial part of any social media analytic capability and has explored various technical approaches.

---

[1]   According to DHS, 2016b, p. 1,

> In 2007, the U.S. Department of State (DOS) began embedding a computer chip in all newly issued U.S. passports (known as electronic passports or "e-Passports,") as part of an overall effort to prevent imposters from using valid U.S. passports to enter the United States.

Summary

FRTs are being increasingly implemented in multiple sectors and across different levels of government. As a result, no unified set of rules governs their use; instead, multiple laws and regulations create a disjointed policy environment, limiting the extent to which privacy and bias concerns can be mitigated for these implementations. Addressing these gaps might require more-specific information in each of the sectors in which FRTs are deployed. Chapter Four describes these considerations in further detail for two security-related use cases: border control and airport surveillance.

Face Recognition Technologies in Action: Two Use Cases

In this chapter, we examine two use cases for how FRTs could be deployed for security purposes that occupy opposite points in the heuristic described in Table 2.1: border control passport authentication and face-in-a-crowd airport surveillance. The former involves low privacy risk and high accuracy, while the latter involves high privacy risk and low accuracy. In each use case, we draw on the research summarized in previous chapters to describe the challenges and opportunities about privacy and PETs (including hacks) and bias. These use cases are deliberately generic to illustrate the privacy and bias issues and the actions that might be taken to mitigate them. It should be noted that DHS is actively working to address these issues, such as by incorporating FIPPs (e.g., transparency, limited data retention) into its border checkpoint technology demonstrations (DHS, 2018b).

Use Case 1: Border Control Passport Authentication

This use case describes a generic airport passport control scenario in which the objective is to confirm that the traveler's face is the same as that in the passport photo. A traveler at a border control point typically presents a passport or other identification that contains a picture to confirm their identity. Some international airports have implemented FRTs to compare information from an electronic passport, which is scanned, with a headshot photo that is taken at the border control point. Typically, this initial comparison takes place during the primary inspection. From there, a border control agent might decide to refer the traveler to secondary inspection if they judge either that there is no FRT match or that the traveler might pose a potential risk. In secondary inspection, the headshot photo might undergo more-rigorous checks or be stored more securely.

This FRT use case can involve another function, beyond its primary purpose of confirming identity: It can match a traveler's information to that on a blacklist (e.g., a terrorist watch list) of people not allowed to enter a territory or subject to further questioning. Such a procedure changes the potential architecture of data storage and introduces additional considerations for privacy, accuracy, and redress. For instance, blacklist matching increases the amount of information needed and secondary use of the data, which might require a secure connection to sensitive databases. Overall, this use-case example highlights how additional features of the system increase complexity and vulnerability.

Privacy Rights and Privacy-Enhancing Technologies

This case is less privacy-invasive than other potential FRT deployments because people know when and where they provide personal data. Thus, they have some measure of control over how their data are used. However, the risks from an FRT match error or privacy invasion can be harmful, including through arrests, physical searches, or delayed travel. As described in the rest of this section, PETs offer several opportunities to protect privacy in this use case.

Data Protection

Implementation or deployment features can include appropriate dataset design that separates information into different storage locations. The blacklist should be stored in a database and server different from those storing the passport identity information. Separating the databases does not offer foolproof protection against a hacker accessing both and linking the information, but it does increase the burden of accessing such information illegitimately, in that more servers and credentials would need to be breached. Similarly, transaction records or logs of the events should be stored in distinct databases with access controls that are different from those storing the PII on the passport.

This will encapsulate access control for authorized personnel and will create a hurdle for malicious users who wish to access and link both sets of information.

Integrity of the image data is important for accurate and trustworthy processing and to ensure the quality of the image taken of the traveler. Image-taking kiosks should be monitored by agents to ensure against the use of physical hacks.

Data Minimization

Data minimization often refers to reducing the need to maintain data, link to other data, or make PII available. However, in this use case, the FRT system is specifically designed to link PII to a face. Opportunities for data minimization include storing only certain elements of the passport application and limiting access to the data. In this case, only passport information needed explicitly for the match is available to the airport system (for instance, passport number, extracted face image features, and perhaps the traveler's name); blacklist matching might require additional information.

Data minimization techniques could include transmitting and storing only extracted and hashed features after an image has been processed, as opposed to transmitting and storing the complete image. One possibility is to do this locally on the equipment taking the image. The trade-off is that doing so removes the possibility for humans to verify or retest the match.

Data Transparency and Correctability

In this case, the traveler is an active participant in the FRT process for all components of the image capture. The traveler is likely aware that having their passport scanned and an image taken means that the two images will be compared and their identity will be verified. A long-form privacy policy at this point might not be desirable, but some information about data protection could be made available if the traveler has any options or choices about it. For instance, in FRT demonstrations, DHS has provided travelers with short-form information and opt-out options (DHS, 2018b).

However, an infrequent or naive traveler might not be aware of the blacklist component of the system. This would likely be considered a secondary use of the data, which might be surprising to travelers and seen as a privacy invasion. Imagine that an innocent traveler enters their own passport in good faith, but the system returns a false positive. Such an error could lead to real harms if people are physically detained or searched or have any of their items confiscated. Notice is also particularly important for redress; travelers cannot address errors if they have no information about the system that is generating errors. Travelers who understand which step of the verification produced the error might be better able to cooperate and provide further materials.

A common concern about system transparency is that bad actors could use any knowledge gained about the system to game it. For instance, if removing one's glasses successfully resolves a failed match, this could suggest that wearing glasses can be an effective hack for automated kiosks, although not when a border control officer is present (e.g., when travelers are referred to secondary inspection). In this use case, it is not clear that any of the possible hacks to this system is exacerbated by notice: Persistent malicious travelers might already assume that the blacklist component exists or might know that they are on the blacklist.

Hacks

When traveling through airports, someone wanted for committing a crime might seek to adopt an identity that will not arouse the suspicion of authorities. To do so, they might employ hacks that they believe are most likely to bypass security systems. In response, authorities would likely upgrade their systems, such as by implementing stricter security protocols that could affect the time that an innocent person spends confirming their identity.

Because most border control access points are operated by humans, perpetrators are unlikely to "spoof" another identity by using photographs, videos, or 3-D masks while a picture is taken. However, several countries are installing systems that outsource identity verification tasks to automated kiosks.[1] In these cases, would-be infiltrators

---

[1] For instance, Customs and Border Protection's Global Entry program uses automated kiosks at which an impersonator would also need to spoof a set of fingerprints.

might not only bypass human interaction but also have more freedom to impersonate an identity by using photographs or video.

In scenarios in which headshots are not taken, criminals could attempt to avoid blacklist matching by using morphing. In other words, the picture used by a criminal in a travel document can be combined with that of a similar-looking person. The advantage of this technique is that the facial characteristics can look sufficiently similar to the unaided eye of a border control agent and bypass FRT blacklist warning systems.

Bias

Differing potential for bias can arise within the passport authentication process. A traveler at a checkpoint poses for a facial photo, which is compared with the passport photo (i.e., one-to-one matching) and potentially against a criminal or terrorist watch list—that is, a database of facial images (i.e., one-to-many matching). When FRTs are applied to match the checkpoint photo to the passport photo, the risk of bias lies in two domains. First, the training data used to build the FRT algorithm might have under- or overrepresented certain groups. This would result in uneven odds that the FRT would return a true positive match, thereby increasing the likelihood that certain groups of travelers are denied benefits (i.e., entry into the country).

The second possibility of bias for direct checkpoint and passport matching is in the human interpretation of the results. Depending on how they are presented (e.g., simple score versus match/no-match judgment), the passport control agent might need to make a final determination on whether to accept the algorithm's recommendation and allow entry. The agent's confidence in making a decision based on the algorithm's recommendation can depend on a subjective judgment about whether the photos match and either implicit or explicit bias about people of certain groups.

Comparing a checkpoint photo with those in a watch-list database of facial images can introduce additional risk of bias in the target data set (i.e., the watch-list database). Certain groups are overrepresented in the watch-list facial database, such as racial minorities who are arrested at disproportionately high rates (Garvie, Bedoya, and Frankle, 2016).

Those groups would be more likely to show positive facial matches, flagging them as high-risk travelers and increasing the likelihood that they would be denied entry to the country.

Even if an FRT system has high-quality training data and has been tested extensively for bias and fairness, the mere existence of an FRT checkpoint could have a chilling effect on travel. Minority or historically persecuted groups might have lower trust in governmental technologies, and the existence of a checkpoint where one needs to present oneself and consent to photo identification and facial matching could deter certain people from traveling. Therefore, transparency and notice about FRT systems might need to be particularly careful about allaying these concerns.

Red Flag Summary

In this use case, these potential red flags indicate concerns about privacy and fairness:

- Adding a secondary use for images beyond authentication increases the complexity of the system. This increases the burden to secure the data and makes data minimization difficult.
- There is a lack of easy redress when errors occur. If the person whose image is being matched cannot easily correct or seek redress when errors occur, the system could be perceived as unfair, and the individuals will not be able to protect their privacy.
- The training data are a possible source of bias. The watch-list training information might not be representative of the travelers, and this could introduce bias.
- When there is no human review of FRT results, hacks involving photographs, videos, or physical masks are possible.
- When headshots are not taken, hacks involving morphing can be attempted.

Use Case 2: Face-in-a-Crowd Airport Surveillance

Around 41,000 people pass through Panama's Tocumen airport each day (Aeropuerto Internacional de Tocumen, 2017). Unbeknownst to most travelers, when they cross one of the 149 terminal cameras capable of capturing their facial characteristics, their image will be compared to those in a database that contains the information of people with national and international arrest warrants (Määttä, Hadid, and Pietikäinen, 2012). This is an example of a many-to-many identification mechanism, whereby faces in a crowd are cross-referenced against a database. In addition, a traveler is not given the opportunity to consent to the use of their likeness for analysis.

The Tocumen FRT system (FaceFirst Guardian, a commercial offering) advertises the ability to find up to 30 suspects each day. This means that an extremely low base rate of 30 out of 41,000 passengers should be marked as suspects each day. Therefore, the FRT system must exhibit an extremely high confidence and accuracy rate, because a sample 99-percent rate would generate more than 400 false positives each day.

Several aspects of how FaceFirst Guardian is used at the Tocumen airport would be relevant to consider for other airports. First, a proprietary commercial technology handles major components of the FRT system. This is relevant for the issue of security, including where information is stored and what information would be duplicated. Second, humans bear responsibility to act on FRT results. Once a match is identified, an alert is sent to agents in the airport that likely includes the matched photos, the location of the person, and possibly other identifying information. At this point, the agent would rely on human face recognition abilities to identify the suspect within the crowded airport. Third, the cameras that collect crowd images are placed at chokepoints, such as escalators. This is likely because travelers will be moving at a slower pace at the time the picture is taken, thus allowing better image quality. Also, if a match is identified, the suspect will more likely be hemmed in or moving slowly, giving human agents more time to respond before the suspect travels to another part of the airport.

Privacy Rights and Privacy-Enhancing Technologies
Compared with the first use case, this one is privacy-invasive, in that it does not give the user any control over how data about them are used. Furthermore, the risks of such invasions can be harmful, including arrests, physical searches, or delayed travel. In this scenario, PETs offer some opportunities to protect privacy.

Data Protection
Airport FRTs likely match people in surveillance footage to those in a centralized database of images and information about suspects collected from national and international law enforcement agencies. Given the sensitive nature of this database, it might be subject to advanced persistent threats, particularly if criminal organizations or other nefarious actors wish to change or modify the data (i.e., to remove or replace images). Therefore, a high level of security is needed for both the data in this database and the data inputs into the system. To allow for redress and to verify its adequate operation, the system will need to keep logs of transactions and decisions. These should be carefully protected and, to the extent possible, scrubbed of PII.

Data Minimization
Real-time deletion of a photo that does not have a match could be advisable. A database that stores travelers' images can include sensitive information, which could be at risk from malicious users who wish to attack the airport system by assessing crowds and flow. Furthermore, travelers might wish to have their travel information secure against business competitors, stalkers, or other motivated attacks on this database. Therefore, it would be sensible to store images of travelers for only a short period of time. A photo that is matched to a suspect would likely need to be kept longer so that law enforcement agents can react and review them.

In the previous use-case example, we discussed the possibility of storing and sharing only the extracted face features instead of the full image. In this case, we note that, if law enforcement or security agencies must search the airport for a suspect based on an image, the full image will be stored and analyzed. This means that the system objectives eliminate at least one privacy-enhancing option.

Data Transparency and Correctability

The nature of this system implies relatively few opportunities for providing notice. Pictures are collected without cooperation from the subjects; this is because airport system designers can choose to hide cameras if they believe that the risk of a suspect evading one is greater than the benefits to travelers of being aware of their presence. Images of suspects might have been captured if someone were under arrest, but images might have also been collected through social media or surveillance cameras.

The issues of access and redress are particularly complicated in the case of false positives. Innocent travelers might not be aware if their photos are included in the suspect database. Once they become aware, they should have an option to dispute the inclusion. Also, as noted above, there is an extremely low base rate of true positives, and there could be hundreds of false positives each day. If the FRT matches a traveler against a suspect, the system for redress (e.g., showing identity documents to an agent) should be accessible and efficient.

Hacks

To avoid detection by FRT-enabled camera networks, people can opt for temporary or permanent methods of disguise. Such methods might be suited to public, noncontrolled environments where subjects are not required to consent to pose for photos. Temporary disguises—hats, glasses, fake facial hair, or makeup—are flexible in that they are interchangeable and easily applied between a person's face and camera lens. Those disguises that can cover greater surface area will leave less information that can link a person's identity to a photo. Permanent detection avoidance can include such options as facial surgery. Its benefit is that it makes artificial barriers unnecessary. However, if an individual's new facial features are discovered and catalogued by FRTs, further surgery or temporary disguises could be necessary to avoid detection.

Bias

General airport surveillance of "faces in the crowd" amounts to conducting numerous unconsented many-to-many matches. Moreover, the process by which the Panama airport case executes FRT matching relies heavily on human involvement because agents are expected to use the results of the FRT to identify and intervene with actual people. This large-scale, multiphase process allows several forms of potential bias. In this use case, bias concerns are related mainly to false positives—that is, certain groups of people being disproportionately matched to law enforcement or airport security databases and then prevented from traveling. In the passport checkpoint example, harm can arise if certain people are disproportionately denied entry because of either false negatives in matching (e.g., person is deemed not to be using a matching passport) or false positives (e.g., person is falsely matched to someone on a watch list).

False positives can arise from bias either in algorithm training data or in the target data to which the faces in the crowd are matched. In particular, target databases are a prime concern for bias in this example, given the disproportionate presence of minorities in law enforcement databases (e.g., mug shots) (Garvie, Bedoya, and Frankle, 2016). Of note is that this research pertains mainly to U.S. databases; results in populations from other countries could differ.

The lack of consent to perform facial matching constitutes another source of potential bias. Under nonideal photo situations (e.g., occluded face, lighting and angle differences), algorithms need to normalize photos, which can introduce additional features where, for example, biased training data can play a role. Bias related to lack of consent can also arise if those who are affected by biased results of facial matching have no knowledge of it and thus no recourse. For instance, if airport agents interviewing people who have been identified using FRTs are more likely to flag minority group members as suspicious, unwarranted precautions could be recorded in their file and then associated with minorities' facial photos. If the data are subsequently used as the basis of either training or target FRT data, either through manual involvement or through bias in FRT results, bias could be created in derivative data sets.

Given that agents are tasked with matching facial photos with people in a proscribed area (i.e., a limited one-to-many match), human involvement can lead to biased end results of the overall FRT process. As noted earlier, human observers evince a variety of biases, such as being better at matching faces of one's own race (i.e., "other-race" effect) (Wells and Olson, 2001; Connelly, 2015; Hourihan, Benjamin, and Liu, 2012), as well as a variety of implicit and explicit stereotypes by race, gender, religion, or sexual orientation. Any of these biases could lead to disproportionate traveler disruption.

The large scale of this airport surveillance amplifies the potential impact of bias. Many-to-many matches have higher error rates than either one-to-one or one-to-many matching (Liu et al., 2015). Yet, even if error rates were small, the absolute number of misidentified people who were then apprehended and questioned would amount to a significant overall disruption to the traveling population, likely disproportionately affecting certain groups.

Finally, like with individual checkpoints, the presence of mass surveillance can deter minorities from acting or behaving freely in public places. If members of these groups do not feel free to engage in normal behaviors (e.g., eating, shopping) in airport surroundings or even to enter such surroundings, they could suffer adverse impact on their freedom to travel.

Red Flag Summary

In this use case, we have identified some potential red flags that indicate concerns about privacy and fairness:

- Although consent and control are necessary aspects of privacy protections, the system offers little or no option for notice or choice.
- If the person whose image is being matched cannot correct or seek redress when errors occur, the system will be considered unfair, and people will not be able to protect their privacy.
- The training data are a possible source of bias. The watch-list training information might not be representative of the travelers, and this can introduce bias.
- The base rate of potential matches is extremely low. Having a large number of false positives can be costly to handle and create distrust in the system.
- Human interpretation of the results introduces more bias and requires the additional storage of full-face images or video.

- Temporary means of masking identity (e.g., hats, glasses, makeup) are well-suited for large, crowded environments, such as airports.

Summary

The two use cases described in this chapter involve comparable environments—both are in airports—but occupy opposite points on the heuristic described in Table 2.1. Therefore, they differ in their potential privacy and bias concerns; accordingly, nefarious actors are likely to attempt different hacks. We noted red flags or elements of both systems that can introduce privacy and bias concerns. This suggests that some common red flags (that could generalize to other FRT uses) were

- a lack of accessible redress when errors occur
- the training and target data being possible sources of bias.

Each use case illustrates more-specific red flags as well. In the first one, feature creep beyond the one-to-one match introduces complexity to the system. Such complexity generates privacy concerns. In the second use case, additional red flags include the following:

- Although consent and control are necessary aspects of privacy protections, the system offers little or no option for notice or choice.
- The base rate of potential matches is extremely low.
- Human interpretation of the results introduces more bias and requires the additional storage of full-face images or video.

These red flags could be applied to other FRT use cases. Further analysis could extend the breadth (i.e., more use cases) and the depth (examining each use case in more detail) beyond analysis of these two use cases.

CHAPTER FIVE

Study Overview and Areas for Future Research

Study Overview

An arms race is brewing between organizations investing in increasing the accuracy and acceptability of face recognition systems and those attempting to undermine the technology through hacks (Galbally, Marcel, and Fierrez, 2014). This study was an initial attempt at a multidimensional exploration of the challenges and implications arising from FRT deployments, particularly for people who are invariably affected by how such technology is employed.

We focused on issues that government organizations should consider when implementing FRTs. Following a literature review and case studies, we identified two broad sets of considerations and lessons. The first of these involves how to ensure the privacy of people subject to these systems. Any technology that gathers PII, such as facial characteristics, in public settings should strive to protect those data, use anonymization or other means to reduce the amount of those data available, and establish rigorous user protocols to limit unauthorized access.

A second area involves bias concerns in the application of this technology. We examined how FRTs can discriminate against groups that share physical characteristics. The composition and size of either training or targeting data sets should be carefully considered to discern the potential for skewing FRT algorithms.

These conceptual themes were investigated further in two use cases: a border control scenario, in which a user volunteers their image for one-to-one authentication, and a faces-in-a-crowd surveillance scenario, in which people are unaware that their identities are subject to some-to-many surveillance. In both, it might be necessary to design blacklists that avoid bias. There is also a need to identify thresholds that produce acceptable rates of false-positive facial matches in security-related applications. Adjusting thresholds is a key policy question that must be addressed in FRT implementations. For instance, if thresholds are set to produce very few false negatives (i.e., no bad actors escape detection), the number of false positives could be very large, requiring significant human efforts to resolve. On the other hand, if thresholds seek to reduce false positives to reduce the burden, the result would be more false negatives, which risks the system becoming useless as a security measure.

Finally, implementing FRT technologies for government use can be best thought of as part of an overall system that includes human judgment and actions. The use-case analysis results illustrate that human agents are fundamental in successfully applying FRTs by either monitoring automated immigration checkpoints against hacking or capturing a suspect identified by the technology.

Areas for Future Research

This study constituted a preliminary effort to survey the privacy and bias challenges in implementing FRTs by government agencies. Further research should address areas of opportunity in the implementation of this technology for security purposes. In particular, the following research directions could deliver significant contributions to fair and accurate FRT implementation:

- **Characterize disparate FRT privacy and bias practices at the local, state, and federal levels.** Many public entities are seeking to complement security efforts with the use of FRTs. Unlike the federal government, state and local government agencies implement heterogeneous standards to protect people from bias and privacy concerns. To better understand the state of FRT policies throughout the country, including where gaps exist, case studies could be used to contrast the varying levels of attention devoted to these issues. Text extraction of public comments (e.g., social media) and clustering techniques could then identify common principles or policy gaps that FRT implementations would need to consider and for which they would need to plan. The findings could help inform, for instance, PIAs for future government adoption of new technologies.

- **Evaluate relevant DHS policies and processes.** Along with other federal agencies, DHS has begun to test and implement FRTs and has released PIAs and policies that document and guide implementation processes. These documents should be evaluated to understand the extent to which they—individually and collectively—address concerns related to privacy and bias. A systematic review of PIAs would catalog, for example, PETs and other FRT program features that aim to safeguard privacy and civil liberties. The review should also identify gaps, such as whether the proposed processes would be adequate for future FRTs. A comprehensive evaluation should also explore what kind of assessment standards are appropriate; there are multiple fairness norms that could shape how to think about the impact of bias.

- **Identify appropriate types and conditions for implementing PETs.** Given that multiple types of PETs exist, there is a need to identify the strengths and weaknesses of each, as well as when they should be used for security implementations to protect privacy. This could begin, for instance, by determining the adoption rates of various PETs either empirically (e.g., environmental scan of FRT implementations) or theoretically (e.g., presenting people with theoretical choices of PETs). Qualitative research could probe about specific barriers to adoption, such as lack of access or desire among the public for specific PETs. Research could also focus on private-sector incentives for developing PETs—for example, whether certain PETs require trade-offs, such as inhibiting companies from being able to make use of valuable digital data that have been collected. Finally, experimental studies involving security use cases could sequentially implement and then substitute various PETs to identify which ones were more frequently adopted or more positively perceived.

- **Evaluate the privacy and bias effects that algorithmic transparency has on FRT implementations.** Algorithmic transparency is increasingly recognized as a way to guard against biased outcomes and to ensure that the results of algorithmic decisionmaking are explainable. Yet transparency in algorithms can involve a performance trade-off and could increase their vulnerability to hacking by exposing the FRT to more-effective adversarial attacks. Moreover, intellectual property concerns might prevent or discourage companies from openly sharing information about their offerings. Empirical research could seek to quantify the extent to which hacking risk increases by sequentially exposing various parts of the FRT system. An alternative to algorithmic transparency could be to focus on algorithmic explainability—that is, establishing how to present and explain how an algorithm operates so that a human can understand, while attempting to minimize the exposure of algorithmic features that could render it vulnerable to hacks.

- **Determine training and target data representativeness for relevant populations (e.g., travelers).** To mitigate the potential for bias, government agencies should seek to ensure that data sets are representative of relevant populations. In passport checkpoints, for instance, both the training data used to train FRTs and the targeting watch lists might be unrepresentative of the demographics of the traveling public. The composition and size of both training and target data sets should be scrutinized to identify thresholds and heuristics that minimize the potential for harm and thresholds of harms that the public will find acceptable. This investigation should also explore whether population segments other than the under- or overrepresented groups are being harmed.

- **Identify privacy and bias considerations in the government acquisition of FRTs.** Officials charged with procuring FRT systems for public agencies are responsible for acquiring solutions that address the needs and concerns of diverse internal and external constituencies. Through interviews and focus groups with acquisition officials or other analyses of acquisition processes, decisionmakers could gain valuable insights from gathering and consolidating the bias and privacy issues considered during the acquisition process.

- **Assemble a centralized repository of FRT accuracy and implications for bias.** A centralized repository of FRT accuracy information based on systematic review of academic literature, commercial offerings, and FRT evaluations (such as those conducted by the National Institute of Standards and Technology) would collect the most up-to-date accuracy rates of existing FRT algorithms and systems. Policymakers can benefit from this information in two ways. First, they would gain a resource that aggregates information on known characteristics of available technology. Second, the data can compare and contrast the implications that these effects could have for identifying people with diverse demographic characteristics.
- **Explore the privacy expectations of FRT targets.** An examination of the social expectations of privacy across diverse societal groups would inform policymakers about the public's concerns in using FRT. Considering that privacy is viewed differently in different spaces (e.g., airport versus public parks), such a study could survey targets in a variety of settings and with varying degrees of invasiveness, similar to the Public Perception of Security and Privacy: Assessing Knowledge, Collecting Evidence, Translating Research into Action survey in 27 European Union countries (Patil et al., 2015). The results from this work could inform how programs are deployed (e.g., messaging) in a manner that addresses the public's concerns about how these technologies affect their privacy.

Bibliography

ACLU—*See* American Civil Liberties Union.

ACLU of Arkansas—*See* American Civil Liberties Union of Arkansas.

Aeropuerto Internacional de Tocumen, *Annual Report 2016*, c. 2017. As of March 31, 2018:
http://tocumenpanama.aero/transparencia/data_2017/Otros/pdf/annual_report_2016_aitsa.pdf

Akhtar, Zahid, and Gian Luca Foresti, "Face Spoof Attack Recognition Using Discriminative Image Patches," *Journal of Electrical and Computer Engineering*, Vol. 2016, art. 4721849.

Alaska State Legislature, an act related to biometric information, 30th Legislature, House Bill 72, January 20, 2017. As of December 30, 2019:
https://www.akleg.gov/basis/Bill/Detail/30?Root=HB%20%2072

Ali, Amal Seralkhatem Osman, Vijanth Sagayan, Aamir Malik, and Azrina Aziz, "Proposed Face Recognition System After Plastic Surgery," *IET Computer Vision*, Vol. 10, No. 5, 2016, pp. 342–348.

Amazon Web Services, "The Facts on Facial Recognition with Artificial Intelligence," undated. As of February 18, 2019:
https://aws.amazon.com/rekognition/the-facts-on-facial-recognition-with-artificial-intelligence/

American Civil Liberties Union, "About the ACLU," undated. As of November 19, 2018:
https://www.aclu.org/about-aclu

American Civil Liberties Union of Arkansas, "ACLU of Arkansas Warns Schools of Privacy Risks of Biometric Surveillance Systems," press release, March 16, 2018. As of August 17, 2018:
https://www.acluarkansas.org/en/press-releases/aclu-arkansas-warns-schools-privacy-risks-biometric-surveillance-systems

American Civil Liberties Union of New York, "NYCLU Urges State to Block Facial Recognition Technology in Lockport Schools," press release, June 18, 2018. As of August 17, 2018:
https://www.nyclu.org/en/press-releases/
nyclu-urges-state-block-facial-recognition-technology-lockport-schools

American National Standards Institute, "CTA: Consumer Technology Association," undated. As of November 19, 2019:
https://webstore.ansi.org/sdo/cta

Angwin, Julia, Jeff Larson, Surya Mattu, and Lauren Kirchner, "Machine Bias," *ProPublica*, May 23, 2016. As of January 30, 2020:
https://www.propublica.org/article/
machine-bias-risk-assessments-in-criminal-sentencing

Barocas, Solon, and Andrew D. Selbst, "Big Data's Disparate Impact," *California Law Review*, Vol. 104, No. 3, June 2016, pp. 671–732.

Barth, Adam, Anupam Datta, John C. Mitchell, and Helen Nissenbaum, "Privacy and Contextual Integrity: Framework and Applications," *Proceedings of the 2006 IEEE Symposium on Security and Privacy*, 2006.

Bass, Katy Glenn, *Chilling Effects: NSA Surveillance Drives U.S. Writers to Self-Censor*, New York: PEN American Center, November 12, 2013. As of December 31, 2019:
https://pen.org/research-resources/chilling-effects/

Brandom, Russell, "How Facial Recognition Helped Police Identify the *Capital Gazette* Shooter," *The Verge*, June 29, 2018. As of December 23, 2019:
https://www.theverge.com/2018/6/29/17518364/
facial-recognition-police-identify-capital-gazette-shooter

Buolamwini, Joy, and Timnit Gebru, "Gender Shades: Intersectional Accuracy Disparities in Commercial Gender Classification," *Proceedings of Machine Learning Research*, Vol. 81, 2018, pp. 77–91.

Center for Democracy and Technology, "About," undated. As of November 19, 2019:
https://cdt.org/about/

Chappellet-Lanier, Tajha, "Department of State to Award Sole Source Facial Recognition Contract," *FedScoop*, June 8, 2018. As of August 22, 2018:
https://www.fedscoop.com/state-department-facial-recognition-idemia/

Cho, Miyoung, and Youngsook Jeong, "Face Recognition Performance Comparison Between Fake Faces and Live Faces," *Soft Computing*, Vol. 21, No. 12, June 2017, pp. 3429–3437.

City and County of San Francisco, Board of Supervisors, "Administrative Code: Acquisition of Surveillance Technology," proposed ordinance, c. 2019. As of December 23, 2019:
https://www.documentcloud.org/documents/
5699972-ORD-Acquisition-of-Surveillance-Technology.html

Commonwealth of Massachusetts Senate, petition to adopt Senate Bill 120, 191st General Court, an act related to consumer data privacy, joint hearing scheduled for September 23, 2019a. As of December 30, 2019:
https://malegislature.gov/Bills/191/SD341

———, petition to adopt Senate Bill 1385, 191st General Court, an act establishing a moratorium on face recognition and other remote biometric surveillance systems, joint hearing scheduled for October 22, 2019b. As of December 23, 2019:
https://malegislature.gov/Bills/191/SD671

Connelly, Laura, "Cross-Racial Identifications: Solutions to the 'They All Look Alike' Effect," *Michigan Journal of Race and Law*, Vol. 21, No. 1, 2015, art. 5. As of January 30, 2020:
https://repository.law.umich.edu/mjrl/vol21/iss1/5/

Conrat, Maisie, and Richard Conrat, *Executive Order 9066: The Internment of 110,000 Japanese Americans*, Los Angeles: University of California, Los Angeles, Asian American Studies Center Press, 1972.

Consumer Federation of America, "About CFA," undated. As of November 19, 2019:
https://consumerfed.org/about-cfa/

Cranor, Lorrie Faith, "Necessary but Not Sufficient: Standardized Mechanisms for Privacy Notice and Choice," *Journal on Telecommunications and High Technology Law*, Vol. 10, No. 2, Summer 2012, pp. 273–445.

Davis, John S., II, and Osonde A. Osoba, *Privacy Preservation in the Age of Big Data: A Survey*, Santa Monica, Calif.: RAND Corporation, WR-1161, 2016. As of December 30, 2019:
https://www.rand.org/pubs/working_papers/WR1161.html

Davis, Zachary S., and Michael Nacht, eds., *Strategic Latency: Red, White, and Blue—Managing the National and International Security Consequences of Disruptive Technologies*, Livermore, Calif.: Lawrence Livermore National Laboratory, Center for Global Security Research, February 2018. As of January 30, 2020:
https://cgsr.llnl.gov/research/book

Deb, Sopan, and Natasha Singer, "Taylor Swift Said to Use Facial Recognition to Identify Stalkers," *New York Times*, December 13, 2018.

Delaware House of Representatives, an act to amend title 6 of the Delaware code related to personal information privacy, 149th General Assembly, House Bill 350, latest action is introduction of House Amendment 1 to the bill, May 30, 2018. As of December 23, 2019: http://legis.delaware.gov/BillDetail?legislationId=26395

Dennedy, Michelle Finneran, Jonathan Fox, and Thomas R. Finneran, *The Privacy Engineer's Manifesto: Getting from Policy to Code to QA to Value*, New York: Apress Open, 2014.

Dhamecha, Tejas Indulal, Richa Singh, Mayank Vatsa, and Ajay Kumar, "Recognizing Disguised Faces: Human and Machine Evaluation," *PLoS ONE*, Vol. 9, No. 7, 2014, art. e99212. As of December 30, 2019: https://doi.org/10.1371/journal.pone.0099212

DHS—*See* U.S. Department of Homeland Security.

Digital Signage Federation, "Who We Are," undated. As of January 3, 2020: https://www.digitalsignagefederation.org/about/

DOS—*See* U.S. Department of State.

Draper, Kevin, "Madison Square Garden Has Used Face-Scanning Technology on Customers," *New York Times*, March 13, 2018.

Dwoskin, Elizabeth, "Amazon Is Selling Facial Recognition to Law Enforcement—for a Fistful of Dollars," *Washington Post*, May 22, 2018. As of December 23, 2019: https://www.washingtonpost.com/news/the-switch/wp/2018/05/22/amazon-is-selling-facial-recognition-to-law-enforcement-for-a-fistful-of-dollars

Edmunds, Taiamiti, and Alice Caplier, "Motion-Based Countermeasure Against Photo and Video Spoofing Attacks in Face Recognition," *Journal of Visual Communication and Image Representation*, Vol. 50, January 2018, pp. 314–332.

Electronic Frontier Foundation, "About EFF," undated. As of November 19, 2019: https://www.eff.org/about

FBI—*See* Federal Bureau of Investigation.

Federal Bureau of Investigation, "Interstate Photo System [Page]," 2015.

Federal Trade Commission, "Complying with COPPA: Frequently Asked Questions," March 20, 2015. As of August 21, 2018: https://www.ftc.gov/tips-advice/business-center/guidance/complying-coppa-frequently-asked-questions

Fenster, Tim, "Local School Districts Look to Security Cameras for Safety," *Niagara Gazette*, March 3, 2018. As of August 17, 2018: http://www.niagara-gazette.com/news/local_news/local-school-districts-look-to-security-cameras-for-safety/article_82e2b2a8-774d-534a-a747-d1df3a00872e.html

Fort Bend Independent School District, "Safety and Security Master Plan," December 6, 2019. As of August 17, 2018:
http://www.fortbendisd.com/site/Default.aspx?PageID=936

Galbally, Javier, Sébastien Marcel, and Julien Fierrez, "Biometric Antispoofing Methods: A Survey in Face Recognition," *IEEE Access*, Vol. 2, 2014, pp. 1530–1552. As of December 30, 2019:
https://ieeexplore.ieee.org/abstract/document/6990726

Garrow, David J., *The FBI and Martin Luther King, Jr.: From "Solo" to Memphis*, New York: Open Road Integrated Media, 2015.

Garvie, Clare, Alvaro Bedoya, and Jonathan Frankle, "The Perpetual Line-Up: Unregulated Police Face Recognition in America," Georgetown University Law Center, Center on Privacy and Technology, October 18, 2016. As of August 20, 2018:
https://www.perpetuallineup.org/

Gellman, Robert, *Fair Information Practices: A Basic History*, version 2.19, Washington, D.C., October 7, 2019. As of January 30, 2020:
https://bobgellman.com/rg-docs/rg-FIPshistory.pdf

Global Justice Information Sharing Initiative, *Face Recognition Policy Development Template for Use in Criminal Intelligence and Investigative Activities*, Bureau of Justice Assistance, U.S. Department of Justice, last revised December 4, 2017. As of December 23, 2019:
https://it.ojp.gov/GIST/1204/Face-Recognition-Policy-Development-Template-For-Use-In-Criminal-Intelligence-and-Investigative-Activities

Gold, Michael, and Bob Braun, "Illinois Expands Protection of Biometric Information: Who's Next? Opening the Gates to Expensive Class Actions and 'Sue and Settle' Lawsuits," *Cybersecurity Lawyer Forum*, January 30, 2019. As of January 30, 2020:
https://cybersecurity.jmbm.com/category/litigation/

Google, "Google Flu Trends," undated. As of January 2, 2020:
https://www.google.org/flutrends/about/

GovTribe, "Land Border Biometric Exit Facial Recognition," federal contract opportunity listing, January 18, 2018. As of January 30, 2020:
https://govtribe.com/opportunity/federal-contract-opportunity/land-border-biometric-exit-facial-recognition-70rsat18r00000002

Guo, Guodong, Lingyun Wen, and Shuicheng Yan, "Face Authentication with Makeup Changes," *IEEE Transactions on Circuits and Systems for Video Technology*, Vol. 24, No. 5, 2014, pp. 814–825.

Hourihan, Kathleen L., Aaron S. Benjamin, and Xiping Liu, "A Cross-Race Effect in Metamemory: Predictions of Face Recognition Are More Accurate for Members of Our Own Race," *Journal of Applied Research in Memory and Cognition*, Vol. 1, No. 3, 2012, pp. 158–162.

Illinois Compiled Statutes, Chapter 740, Civil Liabilities; Act 14, Biometric Information Privacy Act, effective October 3, 2008. As of August 22, 2018: http://www.ilga.gov/legislation/ilcs/ilcs3.asp?ActID=3004&ChapterID=57%20

Illman, Erin Jane, "Data Privacy Laws Targeting Biometric and Geolocation Technologies," *Business Lawyer,* Vol. 73, Winter 2017–2018, pp. 191–197. As of December 30, 2019: https://www.bradley.com/-/media/files/insights/publications/2018/01/the_business_lawyer_winter_20172018_issue_data_privacy_laws.pdf

Interactive Advertising Bureau, "Our Story," undated. As of November 19, 2019: https://www.iab.com/our-story/

International Biometrics and Identity Association, "Who We Are," undated. As of November 19, 2019: https://www.ibia.org/who-we-are-ibia

Jozuka, Emiko, "Glasses That Confuse Facial Recognition Systems Are Coming to Japan," *Motherboard,* August 7, 2015. As of April 14, 2018: https://motherboard.vice.com/en_us/article/jp5zy4/glasses-that-confuse-facial-recognition-systems-are-coming-to-japan

Juvonen, Jaana, *School Violence: Prevalence, Fears, and Prevention,* Santa Monica, Calif.: RAND Corporation, IP-219-EDU, 2001. As of December 30, 2019: https://www.rand.org/pubs/issue_papers/IP219.html

Kemelmacher-Shlizerman, Ira, Steven M. Seitz, Daniel Miller, and Evan Brossard, "The MegaFace Benchmark: 1 Million Faces for Recognition at Scale," *2016 IEEE Conference on Computer Vision and Pattern Recognition (CVPR),* 2016, pp. 4873–4882.

Klare, Brendan F., Mark J. Burge, Joshua C. Klontz, Richard W. Vorder Bruegge, and Anil K. Jain, "Face Recognition Performance: Role of Demographic Information," *IEEE Transactions on Information Forensics and Security,* Vol. 7, No. 6, December 2012, pp. 1789–1801.

Kollreider, K., H. Fronthaler, and J. Bigun, "Verifying Liveness by Multiple Experts in Face Biometrics," IEEE Computer Society Conference on Computer Vision and Pattern Recognition Workshops, Anchorage, Alaska, 2008, pp. 1–6.

Köse, Neslihan, and Jean-Luc Dugelay, "Mask Spoofing in Face Recognition and Countermeasures," *Image and Vision Computing,* Vol. 32, No. 10, October 2014, pp. 779–789.

Lai, ChinLun, and ChiuYuan Tai, "A Smart Spoofing Face Detector by Display Features Analysis," *Sensors,* Vol. 16, No. 7, 2016, art. 1136. As of December 30, 2019: https://doi.org/10.3390/s16071136

Lapowsky, Issie, "Schools Can Now Get Facial Recognition Tech for Free. Should They?" *Wired*, July 17, 2018. As of December 30, 2019: https://www.wired.com/story/realnetworks-facial-recognition-technology-schools/

Law Enforcement Imaging Technology Task Force, *Law Enforcement Facial Recognition Use Case Catalog*, IJIS Institute and International Association of Chiefs of Police, March 2019.

Lazer, David, Ryan Kennedy, Gary King, and Alessandro Vespignani, "The Parable of Google Flu: Traps in Big Data Analysis," *Science*, Vol. 343, No. 6176, March 14, 2014, pp. 1203–1205. As of January 30, 2020: https://science.sciencemag.org/content/343/6176/1203

Lerman, Jonas, "Big Data and Its Exclusions," *Stanford Law Review Online*, Vol. 66, September 2013, pp. 55–63. As of December 30, 2019: https://www.stanfordlawreview.org/online/privacy-and-big-data-big-data-and-its-exclusions/

Li, Lei, Paulo Lobato Correia, and Abdenour Hadid, "Face Recognition Under Spoofing Attacks: Countermeasures and Research Directions," *IET Biometrics*, Vol. 7, No. 1, 2018, pp. 3–14.

Li, Stan Z., and Anil K. Jain, eds., *Handbook of Face Recognition*, 2nd ed., London: Springer, 2011.

Liao, Shannon, "Google Wins Dismissal of Facial Recognition Lawsuit over Biometric Privacy Act," *The Verge*, December 29, 2018. As of January 30, 2020: https://www.theverge.com/2018/12/29/18160432/google-facial-recognition-lawsuit-dismissal-illinois-privacy-act-snapchat-facebook

Lim, Hyungjin, and Pamela Wilcox, "Crime-Reduction Effects of Open-Street CCTV: Conditionality Considerations," *Justice Quarterly*, Vol. 34, No. 4, 2017, pp. 597–626.

Liu, Jingtuo, Yafeng Deng, Tao Bai, Zhengping Wei, and Chang Huang, Baide Research Institute of Deep Learning, "Targeting Ultimate Accuracy: Face Recognition via Deep Embedding," last revised July 23, 2015. As of March 1, 2018: https://arxiv.org/abs/1506.07310

Lynch, Jennifer, "Face Off: Law Enforcement Use of Face Recognition Technology," Electronic Frontier Foundation, February 12, 2018. As of January 30, 2020: https://www.eff.org/wp/law-enforcement-use-face-recognition

Määttä, J., A. Hadid, and M. Pietikäinen, "Face Spoofing Detection from Single Images Using Texture and Local Shape Analysis," *IET Biometrics*, Vol. 1, No. 1, 2012, pp. 3–10.

Madden, Mary, and Lee Rainie, *Americans' Attitudes About Privacy, Security and Surveillance*, Washington, D.C.: Pew Research Center, May 20, 2015. As of December 30, 2019:
https://www.pewresearch.org/internet/2015/05/20/
americans-attitudes-about-privacy-security-and-surveillance/

"Magnolia School District Buying Advanced Camera Surveillance Technology for MHS, MJHS," *Magnolia Reporter*, March 13, 2018. As of August 17, 2018:
http://www.magnoliareporter.com/education/
article_3734adf2-2693-11e8-bbc1-97d4c055b608.html

McClellan, Theresa D., "School District Exploring Options to Improve Safety, Security at Schools," *Fort Bend Star*, June 26, 2018. As of August 17, 2018:
http://www.fortbendstar.com/
school-district-exploring-options-to-improve-safety-security-at-schools/

McKamey, Mark, "Legal Technology: Artificial Intelligence and the Future of Law Practice," *Appeal*, Vol. 22, 2017, pp. 45–58.

Means, Jacquelyn M., Ira J. Kodner, Douglas Brown, and Shuddhadeb Ray, "Sharing Clinical Photographs: Patient Rights, Professional Ethics, and Institutional Responsibilities," *Bulletin of the American College of Surgeons*, October 1, 2015. As of December 30, 2019:
http://bulletin.facs.org/2015/10/sharing-clinical-photographs-patient-rights-professional-ethics-and-institutional-responsibilities/

Medioni, Gérard, Jongmoo Choi, Cheng-Hao Kuo, Anustup Choudhury, Li Zhang, and Douglas Fidaleo, *Non-Cooperative Persons Identification at a Distance with 3D Face Modeling*, IEEE International Conference on Biometrics: Theory, Applications, and Systems, 2007, pp. 1–6.

Michigan Legislature, a bill to regulate the acquisition, possession, and protection of biometric identifiers and biometric information by private entities and to provide remedies, House Bill 5019, introduced and referred to committee September 27, 2017. As of December 31, 2019:
http://legislature.mi.gov/doc.aspx?2017-HB-5019

Min, Rui, Abdenour Hadid, and Jean-Luc Dugelay, "Efficient Detection of Occlusion Prior to Robust Face Recognition," *Scientific World Journal*, Vol. 2014, No. 3, January 2014, art. 519158.

Moeini, Ali, Karim Faez, and Hossein Moeini, "Face Recognition Across Makeup and Plastic Surgery from Real-World Images," *Journal of Electronic Imaging*, Vol. 24, No. 5, 2015, art. 053028.

Moniz, Erin, Giulia Righi, Jessie J. Peissig, and Michael J. Tarr, "The Clark Kent Effect: What Is the Role of Familiarity and Eyeglasses in Recognizing Disguised Faces?" *Journal of Vision*, Vol. 10, No. 7, August 2010, art. 615.

Nappi, Michele, Stefano Ricciardi, and Massimo Tistarelli, "Deceiving Faces: When Plastic Surgery Challenges Face Recognition," *Image and Vision Computing*, Vol. 54, October 2016, pp. 71–82.

National Telecommunications and Information Administration, "Privacy Multistakeholder Process: Facial Recognition Technology," June 17, 2016. As of January 3, 2020:
https://www.ntia.doc.gov/other-publication/2016/
privacy-multistakeholder-process-facial-recognition-technology

NetChoice, "About Us," undated. As of March 29, 2019:
https://netchoice.org/about/

Neuburger, Jeffrey, "California Court Refuses to Dismiss Biometric Privacy Suit Against Facebook, *New Media and Technology Law Blog*, May 9, 2016. As of August 22, 2018:
https://newmedialaw.proskauer.com/2016/05/09/
california-court-refuses-to-dismiss-biometric-privacy-suit-against-facebook/

———, "Biometric Privacy Claims over Facial Recognition Feature in Videogame Dismissed for Lack of Concrete Harm," *New Media and Technology Law Blog*, February 2, 2017a. As of August 22, 2018:
https://newmedialaw.proskauer.com/2017/02/02/biometric-privacy-claims-over-
facial-recognition-feature-in-videogame-dismissed-for-lack-of-concrete-harm/

———, "Court Refuses to Dismiss Biometric Privacy Action over Facial Recognition Technology Used by Google Photos," *New Media and Technology Law Blog*, March 2, 2017b. As of August 22, 2018:
https://newmedialaw.proskauer.com/2017/03/02/court-refuses-to-dismiss-
biometric-privacy-action-over-facial-recognition-technology-used-by-google-
photos/

———, "California Court Declines to Dismiss Illinois Facial Recognition/
Biometric Privacy Suit Against Facebook on Standing Grounds," *New Media and Technology Law Blog*, March 2, 2018. As of August 22, 2018:
https://newmedialaw.proskauer.com/2018/03/02/california-court-declines-to-
dismiss-illinois-facial-recognition-biometric-privacy-suit-against-facebook-on-
standing-grounds/

New York State Assembly, Biometric Privacy Act, Senate Bill S01203, referred to consumer protection January 11, 2019. As of December 30, 2019:
https://assembly.state.ny.us/leg/?term=2019&bn=S01203

Nissenbaum, Helen Fay, *Privacy in Context: Technology, Policy, and the Integrity of Social Life*, Stanford, Calif.: Stanford University Press, 2009.

NTIA—*See* National Telecommunications and Information Administration.

Osoba, Osonde A., and William Welser IV, *An Intelligence in Our Image: The Risks of Bias and Errors in Artificial Intelligence*, Santa Monica, Calif.: RAND Corporation, RR-1744-RC, 2017. As of December 31, 2019: https://www.rand.org/pubs/research_reports/RR1744.html

O'Toole, Alice J., P. Jonathon Phillips, Xiaobo An, and Joseph Dunlop, "Demographic Effects on Estimates of Automatic Face Recognition Performance," *Image and Vision Computing*, Vol. 30, No. 3, March 2012, pp. 169–176.

Oulasvirta, Antti, Aurora Pihlajamaa, Jukka Perkiö, Debarshi Ray, Taneli Vähäkangas, Tero Hasu, Niklas Vainio, and Petri Myllymäki, "Long-Term Effects of Ubiquitous Surveillance in the Home," presented at 14th International Conference on Ubiquitous Computing, Pittsburgh, Pa., September 5, 2012.

Palen, Leysia, and Paul Dourish, "Unpacking 'Privacy' for a Networked World," *CHI '03: Proceedings of the SIGCHI Conference on Human Factors in Computing Systems*, April 2003, pp. 129–136.

Parveen, Sajida, Sharifa Mumtazah Syed Ahmad, Marsyita Hanafi, and Wan Azizun Wan Adnan, "Face Anti-Spoofing Methods," *Current Science*, Vol. 108, No. 8, April 25, 2015, pp. 1491–1500.

Patil, Sunil, Bhanu Patruni, Hui Lu, Fay Dunkerley, James Fox, Dimitris Potoglou, and Neil Robinson, *Public Perception of Security and Privacy: Results of the Comprehensive Analysis of PACT's Pan-European Survey*, Santa Monica, Calif.: RAND Corporation, RR-704-EC, 2015. As of December 30, 2019: https://www.rand.org/pubs/research_reports/RR704.html

Penney, Jonathon W., "Chilling Effects: Online Surveillance and Wikipedia Use," *Berkeley Technology Law Journal*, Vol. 31, No. 1, 2016, pp. 117–182.

Phillips, P. Jonathon, Fang Jiang, Abhijit Narvekar, Julianne Ayyad, and Alice J. O'Toole, "An Other-Race Effect for Face Recognition Algorithms," *ACM Transactions on Applied Perception*, Vol. 8, No. 2, February 2011, art. 14.

Phillips, P. Jonathon, Amy N. Yates, Ying Hu, Carina A. Hahn, Eilidh Noyes, Kelsey Jackson, Jacqueline G. Cavazos, Géraldine Jeckeln, Rajeev Ranjan, Swami Sankaranarayanan, Jun-Cheng Chen, Carlos D. Castillo, Rama Chellappa, David White, and Alice J. O'Toole, "Face Recognition Accuracy of Forensic Examiners, Superrecognizers, and Face Recognition Algorithms," *Proceedings of the National Academy of Sciences of the United States of America*, Vol. 115, No. 24, June 12, 2018, pp. 6171–6176.

Public Law 91-508, an act to amend the Federal Deposit Insurance Act to require insured banks to maintain certain records, to require that certain transactions in U.S. currency be reported to the U.S. Department of the Treasury, and for other purposes, October 26, 1970. As of January 2, 2020: https://www.govinfo.gov/app/details/STATUTE-84/STATUTE-84-Pg1114-2

Public Law 93-380, Education Amendments of 1974, August 21, 1974.

Public Law 93-579, Privacy Act of 1974, December 31, 1974. As of January 2, 2020:
https://www.govinfo.gov/app/details/STATUTE-88/STATUTE-88-Pg1896

Public Law 99-474, Computer Fraud and Abuse Act, October 16, 1986. As of January 2, 2020:
https://www.govinfo.gov/app/details/STATUTE-100/STATUTE-100-Pg1213

Public Law 99-508, Electronic Communications Privacy Act of 1986, October 21, 1986. As of January 2, 2020:
https://www.govinfo.gov/app/details/STATUTE-100/STATUTE-100-Pg1848

Public Law 104-191, Health Insurance Portability and Accountability Act of 1996, August 21, 1996. As of January 2, 2020:
https://www.govinfo.gov/app/details/PLAW-104publ191

Public Law 105-277, Omnibus Consolidated and Emergency Supplemental Appropriations Act, 1999, October 21, 1998. As of January 2, 2020:
https://www.govinfo.gov/app/details/PLAW-105publ277

Public Law 106-102, Gramm–Leach–Bliley Act, November 12, 1999. As of January 2, 2020:
https://www.govinfo.gov/app/details/PLAW-106publ102

Public Law 107-296, Homeland Security Act of 2002, November 25, 2002. As of May 12, 2019:
https://www.govinfo.gov/app/details/PLAW-107publ296

Public Law 107-347, E-Government Act of 2002, December 17, 2002. As of January 2, 2020:
https://www.govinfo.gov/app/details/PLAW-107publ347

RealNetworks, "SAFR for K–12 Implementation Best Practices," SAFR Support Center, c. 2018.

Rivera v. Google, 366 F. Supp. 3d 998, N.D. Ill., December 29, 2018.

Roberts, Jeff John, "Walmart's Use of Sci-Fi Tech to Spot Shoplifters Raises Privacy Questions," *Fortune*, November 9, 2015. As of December 30, 2019:
http://fortune.com/2015/11/09/wal-mart-facial-recognition/

Robertson, David J., Robin S. S. Kramer, and A. Mike Burton, "Fraudulent ID Using Face Morphs: Experiments on Human and Automatic Recognition," *PLoS ONE*, Vol. 12, No. 3, March 22, 2017, art. e0173319. As of December 31, 2019:
https://doi.org/10.1371/journal.pone.0173319

Rosenbach v. Six Flags Entertainment Corp., 2019 IL 123186, January 25, 2019. As of January 30, 2020:
https://courts.illinois.gov/Opinions/SupremeCourt/2019/123186.pdf

Rudolph, Harrison, Laura M. Moy, and Alvaro M. Bedoya, *Not Ready for Takeoff: Face Scans at Airport Departure Gates*, Georgetown University Law Center, Center on Privacy and Technology, December 21, 2017. As of December 30, 2019: https://www.law.georgetown.edu/privacy-technology-center/publications/ not-ready-for-takeoff/

Schanz, Jenn, "'Facial Recognition' Software in Lockport City Schools Sparks Concern from NYCLU," WIVB, June 20, 2018.

Schauer, Frederick, "Fear, Risk and the First Amendment: Unraveling the 'Chilling Effect,'" *Boston University Law Review*, Vol. 58, 1978, pp. 685–732.

Sepas-Moghaddam, Alireza, Luis Malhadas, Paulo Lobato Correia, and Fernando Pereira, "Face Spoofing Detection Using a Light Field Imaging Framework," *IET Biometrics*, Vol. 7, No. 1, 2018, pp. 39–48.

Sharif, Mahmood, Sruti Bhagavatula, Lujo Bauer, and Michael K. Reiter, *Accessorize to a Crime: Real and Stealthy Attacks on State-of-the-Art Face Recognition*, CCS '16: Proceedings of the 2016 ACM SIGSAC Conference on Computer and Communications Security, October 2016, pp. 1528–1540. As of December 31, 2019: https://dl.acm.org/doi/10.1145/2976749.2978392

Singh, Richa, Mayank Vatsa, Himanshu S. Bhatt, Samarth Bharadwaj, Afzel Noore, and Shahin S. Nooreyezdan, "Plastic Surgery: A New Dimension to Face Recognition," *IEEE Transactions on Information Forensics and Security*, Vol. 5, No. 3, September 2010, pp. 441–448.

Slovic, Paul, Baruch Fischhoff, and Sarah Lichtenstein, "Facts and Fears: Understanding Perceived Risk," in Richard C. Schwing and Walter A. Albers, eds., *Societal Risk Assessment: How Safe Is Safe Enough?* New York: Springer Science and Business Media, 1980, pp. 181–216.

Smith, Brad, "Facial Recognition: It's Time for Action," *Microsoft on the Issues*, December 6, 2018. As of February 18, 2019: https://blogs.microsoft.com/on-the-issues/2018/12/06/ facial-recognition-its-time-for-action/

State of California, an act to add Title 1.81.5 (commencing with Section 1798.100) to Part 4 of Division 3 of the Civil Code, related to privacy, June 28, 2018. As of December 30, 2019: https://leginfo.legislature.ca.gov/faces/ billTextClient.xhtml?bill_id=201720180AB375

Strauss, Valerie, "And Now, Facial-Recognition Technology Used in Casinos Is Going into a Public School District," *Washington Post*, May 24, 2018. As of August 17, 2018: https://www.washingtonpost.com/news/answer-sheet/wp/2018/05/24/and-now-facial-recognition-technology-used-in-casinos-is-going-into-a-public-school-district/

Texas Business and Commerce Code, Title 11, Personal Identity Information; Subtitle A, Identifying Information; Chapter 503, Biometric Identifiers; Section 503.001, Capture or Use of Biometric Identifier. As of December 31, 2019: https://statutes.capitol.texas.gov/?link=BC

Tufekci, Zeynep, "Algorithmic Harms Beyond Facebook and Google: Emergent Challenges of Computational Agency," *Colorado Technology Law Journal*, Vol. 13, No. 2, 2015, pp. 203–218.

United Nations General Assembly, "Universal Declaration of Human Rights," Resolution 217 A, December 10, 1948. As of December 31, 2019: https://www.un.org/en/universal-declaration-human-rights/

U.S. Army Test and Evaluation Command, *Department of Defense (DOD) Automated Biometric Identification System (ABIS) Version 1.2: Initial Operational Test and Evaluation Report*, Alexandria, Va., May 5, 2015. As of December 30, 2019: http://www.dtic.mil/docs/citations/ADA626558

U.S. Code, Title 6, Domestic Security; Chapter 1, Homeland Security Organization; Subchapter III, Science and Technology in Support of Homeland Security; Section 185, Federally Funded Research and Development Centers. As of May 12, 2019: https://www.govinfo.gov/app/details/USCODE-2017-title6/USCODE-2017-title6-chap1-subchapIII-sec185

U.S. Department of Homeland Security, *Privacy Impact Assessment for the Automated Biometric Identification System (IDENT)*, DHS/NPPD/PIA-002, December 7, 2012. As of August 23, 2018: https://www.dhs.gov/publication/dhsnppdpia-002-automated-biometric-identification-system

———, *Privacy Impact Assessment for the U.S. Customs and Border Protection 1:1 Facial Recognition Air Entry Pilot*, DHS/CBP/PIA-025, March 11, 2015. As of December 31, 2019: https://www.dhs.gov/publication/facial-recognition-air-entry-pilot

———, *Privacy Impact Assessment for the 1-to-1 Facial Comparison Project (Formerly Known as the 1:1 Facial Recognition Air Entry Pilot)*, DHS/CBP/PIA-025(a), January 14, 2016a. As of December 31, 2019: https://www.dhs.gov/publication/facial-recognition-air-entry-pilot

———, *Privacy Impact Assessment Update for the 1-to-1 Facial Comparison Project*, DHS/CBP/PIA-025(b), October 18, 2016b. As of December 31, 2019: https://www.dhs.gov/publication/facial-recognition-air-entry-pilot

———, "Privacy Act of 1974; System of Records," *Federal Register*, Vol. 82, No. 179, September 18, 2017. As of December 30, 2019: https://www.govinfo.gov/app/details/FR-2017-09-18/2017-19365

———, "Land Border Biometric Exit Facial Recognition," *Federal Business Opportunities*, changed January 18, 2018a.

———, *Privacy Impact Assessment Update for the Traveler Verification Service (TVS): CBP-TSA Technical Demonstration Phase II*, DHS/CBP/PIA-030(e), August 14, 2018b. As of December 31, 2019:
https://www.dhs.gov/publication/departure-information-systems-test

———, "Report 2019-01 of the DHS Data Privacy and Integrity Advisory Committee (DPIAC): Privacy Recommendations in Connection with the Use of Facial Recognition Technology," Report 2019-01, February 26, 2019. As of December 30, 2019:
https://www.dhs.gov/publication/dpiac-recommendations-report-2019-01

U.S. Department of Justice, "E-Government Act of 2002," June 16, 2014. Current version, as of August 23, 2018:
https://www.justice.gov/opcl/e-government-act-2002

———, "Privacy Act of 1974," updated July 17, 2015. As of January 31, 2020, current version:
https://www.justice.gov/opcl/privacy-act-1974

U.S. Department of State, *Privacy Impact Assessment (PIA): Automated Biometric Identification System (ABIS)*, version 07.02.04, last updated August 8, 2013. As of December 31, 2019:
https://2009-2017.state.gov/documents/organization/242309.pdf

———, "IBS PIA," July 9, 2015. As of December 31, 2019:
https://2009-2017.state.gov/documents/organization/246821.pdf

U.S. Government Accountability Office, *Facial Recognition Technology: Commercial Uses, Privacy Issues, and Applicable Federal Law*, GAO-15-621, July 30, 2015. As of December 30, 2019:
https://www.gao.gov/products/GAO-15-621

———, *Face Recognition Technology: FBI Should Better Ensure Privacy and Accuracy*, GAO-16-267, reissued August 3, 2016. As of December 30, 2019:
https://www.gao.gov/products/GAO-16-267

———, *DOD Biometrics and Forensics: Progress Made in Establishing Long-Term Deployable Capabilities, but Further Actions Are Needed*, GAO-17-580, August 7, 2017. As of December 30, 2019:
https://www.gao.gov/products/GAO-17-580

Walker, Kent, "AI for Social Good in Asia Pacific," Google, December 13, 2018. As of February 18, 2019:
https://www.blog.google/around-the-globe/google-asia/ai-social-good-asia-pacific/

Washington State Legislature, Concerning Biometric Identifiers, House Bill 1493, governor signed May 16, 2017. As of December 31, 2019:
https://app.leg.wa.gov/
billsummary?BillNumber=1493&Year=2017&Initiative=false

Watanabe, Teresa, and Paloma Esquivel, "L.A. Area Muslims Say FBI Surveillance Has a Chilling Effect on Their Free Speech and Religious Practices," *Los Angeles Times*, March 1, 2009. As of January 30, 2020:
https://www.latimes.com/archives/la-xpm-2009-mar-01-me-muslim1-story.html

Wells, Gary L., and Elizabeth A. Olson, "The Other-Race Effect in Eyewitness Identification: What Do We Do About It?" *Psychology, Public Policy, and Law*, Vol. 7, No. 1, 2001, pp. 230–246.

Welsh, Brandon C., and David P. Farrington, "Public Area CCTV and Crime Prevention: An Updated Systematic Review and Meta-Analysis," *Justice Quarterly*, Vol. 26, No. 4, 2009, pp. 716–745.

Zhang, Le-Bing, Fei Peng, Le Qin, and Min Long, "Face Spoofing Detection Based on Color Texture Markov Feature and Support Vector Machine Recursive Feature Elimination," *Journal of Visual Communication and Image Representation*, Vol. 51, February 2018, pp. 56–69.

Zhuang, Liansheng, Allen Y. Yang, Zihan Zhou, S. Shankar Sastry, and Yi Ma, *Single-Sample Face Recognition with Image Corruption and Misalignment via Sparse Illumination Transfer*, IEEE Conference on Computer Vision and Pattern Recognition, 2013, pp. 3546–3553.

CPSIA information can be obtained
at www.ICGtesting.com
Printed in the USA
BVHW011933210520
580104BV00005B/65